Creating a Responsive Environment for People with Profound and Multiple Learning Difficulties

Jean Ware

David Fulton Publishers
London

David Fulton Publishers Ltd
2 Barbon Close, London WC1N 3JX

First published in Great Britain by
David Fulton Publishers 1996

Note: The right of the author to be identified as the author of this work
has been asserted by her in accordance with the Copyright, Designs and
Patents Act 1988.

Copyright © Jean Ware

British Library Cataloguing in Publication Data

A catalogue record for this book is available from the British Library

ISBN 1-85346-399-X

Typeset by The Harrington Consultancy Ltd.
Printed in Great Britain by the Cromwell Press Ltd, Melksham

Contents

Introduction

About this book

This book is intended for those working with people with profound and multiple learning difficulties (PMLDs), whether as teachers or assistants in school, as instructors in Social Education Centres or as nurses or carestaff in homes or hostels. It is based on a research project funded by the ESRC which ran in two London schools.

When we use the term 'profound and multiple learning difficulties' to describe someone's disability we mean that their degree of learning difficulty is so severe that they are functioning at a developmental level of two years or less (in practice, often well under a year) and also they have one or more other severe impairments, for example they may be unable to walk, be severely visually impaired, or both.

Our intention in writing this book is to enable teachers and carestaff, whether they are working with a group all of whom have PMLDs or with individuals within a generally less severely disabled group, to create for their pupils or clients a particular type of interactive environment, which we call a responsive environment. We think such environments are important for people with PMLDs for several reasons. First, they are positive environments to be in for both pupils/clients and staff. Second, they capitalize on individual strengths which are often ignored, such as the differences in approach, tone of voice etc. between staff members, and the different relationships that develop between staff and pupils/clients.

Thirdly, we also believe that a responsive environment can help children (and adults) with profound and multiple learning difficulties to make progress. We are *not* claiming that such progress will be dramatic. Nor are we claiming that providing a responsive environment is the only way progress can be obtained. Indeed we believe that the work of other researchers also holds exciting prospects for enhancing learning opportunities and quality of life for people with PMLDs. For example the work of Dunst et al in the States and of Sheila Glenn and her colleagues in this country.

Inevitably, because the project was carried out in schools, the examples refer to school age children, but we hope that those who work in other settings will also find them relevant. Teachers and support assistants from schools will not find any references to the National Curriculum because this book is not about curriculum content but about the framework of interactions, whatever their content. That is not to say that the content of what is taught in schools, or the activities which are provided for adults with PMLDs or children outside of school hours are not important, simply that these are areas this book does not attempt to cover.

The first chapter outlines what a responsive environment is and the research that supports our view that it is an appropriate type of environment for people with PMLDs. The next five chapters each look at one aspect of the responsive environment for people with PMLDs and are intended to be 'done' rather than simply read. The final chapter is concerned with how, once you've created a responsive environment in your school or centre, you can help it to last.

'Doing' the book

Ideally each chapter should be worked through at a meeting or meetings between all the relevant staff, because an important aspect of creating a responsive environment is the sharing of information between staff – it really doesn't matter if you've only got half an hour available at lunchtimes every couple of weeks – this book is designed to be used in situations like that. It isn't a good idea to try and cover several chapters during a longer session such as an INSET day, because it's important that you get the chance to try out the ideas one at a time, and get familiar with each before you attempt the next one.

One person will need to agree to be the coordinator, it could be a teacher responsible for pupils with PMLDs; it might in some schools be the speech therapist, since communication is a central aspect of a responsive environment; in a small residential home it could be the person in charge, or it might be the psychologist if one is available to help. The coordinator is responsible for making sure that all the materials needed for a particular session are available, for leading the session, and for giving the other staff involved positive feedback when they try out the ideas suggested. If you decide to implement a responsive environment on a long-term basis the coordinator will also need to monitor it and continue giving the other staff positive feedback about the way they are working.

By all the relevant staff we mean all those who contribute to the interactive environment of the pupils you are concerned with. So if, for example, you run a class specifically for pupils with PMLDs you would want to have present: yourself, all the assistants who work with you, the physio and speech therapist and the school nurse, if any of these people interact regularly with the pupils. You would also want any other school staff who regularly work with your class to be present if at all possible – perhaps they have a music session taken by the music teacher while you take her class for PE – if possible she should come to the sessions where you work through this book. Obviously this is a counsel of perfection, but it is important that all the regular classroom staff should be present if at all possible, even if that means having to make arrangements for someone else to look after the pupils for half an hour or so. If you work in a residential care establishment, it would mean getting together all the staff who have regular contact with the people you are concerned with on the various shifts. Potentially, unless the service in which you work is structured to allow that to happen, that can be very difficult, and you might have to have two groups going through the book separately.

Of course, we're not suggesting that this book isn't worth reading unless you can take part in such a group. We hope that however you use it, it will enhance your work with people with PMLDs, and so make a positive contribution to their lives.

CHAPTER 1

The Importance of a Responsive Environment

Introduction

This chapter is a little different from those that follow because it gives basic information about what a responsive environment is, and looks at the evidence for suggesting that such an environment can be beneficial to people with PMLDs and the staff who work with them.

If you are coordinating a group of people working through the book together, you need to read this chapter before your group meeting, so that you can lead a discussion based on the summary at the end.

What is 'a responsive environment'?

By 'a responsive environment,' we mean an environment in which people get responses to their actions, get the opportunity to give responses to the actions of others, and have an opportunity to take the lead in interaction. There are two ways in which people receive responses to their actions: from other people, and from seeing things happen as a result of what they do. This may sound rather abstract, but some examples should clarify what we mean.

If you speak to a friend, they will probably respond in some way, perhaps by pausing in what they are doing, or by looking at you, or by replying; indicating that they are attending to you. What is more, you behave as if you expect a response from them, pausing after your initial greeting to give them chance to reply.

If you see a colleague approaching a closed door with an armful of equipment and you move to open it for them, they will probably acknowledge your action in some way, perhaps by smiling or by thanking you.

When you turn on the tap, water comes out (unless of course the mains have been switched off). You press the emergency button in your classroom because a child is having a severe fit, and the nurse and headteacher come running.

Similarly, a young infant may start cooing, and attract a response from a nearby adult, they may hear a familiar voice and vocalise; attracting a greeting from the adult in response. The same child may hear the noises of preparation as a drink is being made, and smile in anticipation, again attracting a response from the person who is making the drink. They may hit the mobile attached over their cot, and the toy reacts by moving and making noises. In other words, their actions receive responses.

At another time the child may be lying quiet but alert in their pram, and be asked by a passing adult: 'What are you thinking about, Joe?'. The adult who asks the question, although they are not expecting a verbal reply, pauses in much the same way as if they had been addressing another adult. There is an expectation that the infant will respond, perhaps just by smiling or maybe by cooing; and this may well lead to the conversation being continued. To the smile the adult says: 'It's a secret is it?' and so on.

When you have a discussion with a friend the initiative passes backwards and forwards between you, so that overall neither you nor they dominate the conversation. Perhaps you start the topic – holidays for example; but then they raise the issue of whether you are going to go self-catering or think about a hotel or guesthouse; you raise the possibility of going out of season, they suggest taking others along; you are equal participants in the dialogue. Like conversations, joint activities are most satisfying for both partners when first one takes the lead and then the other. Of course there are exceptions, as when one person has a much higher level of expertise in the activity than the other, this person may dominate that particular activity. In the same way, when an infant and caregiver are playing together, first one and then the other takes the lead, perhaps mum gives the child a toy to play with, and comments as the child examines it; after a few minutes the child's eye is caught by the sun's light reflected in some shiny paper, she vocalises excitedly and this then becomes the focus of mum's attention as well as the child's. When an infant is very young, or the activity is a novel one, the caregiver may dominate the interaction, but as the infant gets older and more skilful he or she quickly becomes an equal partner in the interaction, sometimes being the leader and sometimes following the caregiver's lead.

Why is a responsive environment important?
The research evidence

At one level then, there's nothing very extraordinary about a responsive environment, it's part of the normal experience of most people from birth to adulthood, and particularly of normal, healthy infants in interaction with their mothers (or whoever happens to be their main caregiver). Research on such early interactions shows that, long before the infant has any intention to communicate (in the sense of acting with a deliberate intention to affect someone else's behaviour), adults treat him or her as if their actions had meaning. The example of the adult's response to the alert but quiet baby given above is an example of such behaviour. The evidence suggests that it is through this the infant learns to communicate (e.g. Snow, 1981; 1984; Scoville, 1984). Additionally it has been found that infants who experience a more responsive environment make faster social and cognitive progress. For example, Lewis and Coates (1980) found an association between mothers' responsiveness and the cognitive development of their 12 week old infants, and report that similar associations have been found by other researchers. Of course, such an association does not prove that the mother's responsiveness causes the infant's cognitive gains, it might be that mothers are more responsive to infants who are cognitively advanced.

However, a study by Anderson and Sawin (1983) showed that a simple intervention procedure (having the mother present while a neonatal behaviour assessment was administered and explained) was successful in increasing mothers' responsiveness to their (non-disabled) infants. The infants' responsiveness to their mothers also increased, and they were also more alert and showed more positive affect than infants whose mothers had not received the intervention, although they were only one month old. Anderson and Sawin suggest that the only possible explanation for this change in the infant's behaviour was that it resulted from the mother's increased awareness of how to respond to her infant.

Do people with PMLDs experience a responsive environment?

If then a responsive environment is important for social, communicative and intellectual development, the extent to which such an environment is experienced by people with PMLDs is clearly of interest. Furthermore, since people with PMLDs may well remain in the pre-intentional stages of communication for many years such an environment may continue to be important for them at school or even later in life.

In our initial investigations into what was happening in classrooms for pupils with PMLDs we found that on the whole they had few opportunities for interaction of any sort, and even fewer which gave them the opportunity to participate (Ware and Evans, 1986; Ware, 1987). This was similar to the situation in residential institutions reported earlier by other researchers (e.g. Paton and Stirling 1974; Veit, Allen and Chinsky, 1976). In another observational study of classrooms carried out around the same time as our initial work, Houghton *et al* (1987) found that students with severe disabilities received only very few responses to their initiations expressing choices. By contrast, non-disabled young children functioning at a similar developmental level are active participants in interactions with their caregivers, and this active participation is regarded as important for their development (see above). It would be useful, therefore, to know whether infants with PMLDs also participate actively in early interactions with their caregivers.

Unfortunately, there is very little research which examines the interactive environments experienced by infants with PMLDs; however there is a good deal which compares the interactive environment of groups of infants with a variety of different disabilities with that of non-disabled infants. Looking at these studies, which are reviewed below, can help us to predict the sort of interactive environment likely to be experienced by infants who have PMLDs.

Field (1983) found that 4 month old pre-term infants observed in spontaneous play interaction with their mothers spent more time crying and less time vocalising than 'normal' infants. They were also less likely to smile and/or vocalise in response to their mothers; less likely to look happy and more likely to look sad. Likewise their mothers were more likely to look sad, and less likely to look happy than the mothers of the 'normal' infants. Additionally, they vocalised more, and Field suggests that this represents their attempts to get responses from an unresponsive baby. However the pre-term babies spent more time than the 'normal' infants with their gaze averted from their mothers, in other words it looked as if the mothers' additional efforts were counter-productive.

Similarly, Hanzlik and Stevenson (1986) found that mothers of infants with both cerebral-palsy and learning difficulties demonstrated a higher overall level of behaviour, and a higher level of commands than mothers of non-disabled infants of either the same chronological age (CA) (mean 21 months) or the same mental age (MA) (mean 11.6 months). The cerebral palsied infants, and another group of infants with moderate learning difficulties (but not cerebral-palsy), like those in Field's study had a lower overall level of behaviour than non-disabled infants of the same chronological age, and they also engaged in fewer verbal interactions with their mothers. Furthermore Hanzlik and Stevenson found that the both the infants with cerebral-palsy and learning difficulties and the infants with learning difficulties alone were more likely to be involved in competing behaviour with their mothers than non-disabled infants of either the same CA or the same MA.

Like Field and Hanzlik and Stevenson, Mahoney and Robenalt (1986) compared the interactions of infants with and without disabilities with their mothers during free play. They found that the infants with Down's Syndrome in their study (who had MAs of 15-19 months) 'were less active communicative partners' than a carefully matched group without disabilities. They also found that the mothers of the children with Down's Syndrome were more likely to dominate the interaction rather than mother and infant being more or less equal partners, as was the case with the non-disabled group. That is, the mothers of the Down's Syndrome infants took more turns, gave more commands, and spent less time responding to their children than the mothers of the non-disabled group.

A number of other researchers working with children with a variety of disabilities and their caregivers have similarly found that the caregivers tend to dominate interactions. A study by Garrad (1986) with developmentally delayed preschool children is particularly interesting, because she looked at how interactions developed as the children got older. She found that mothers used more controlling questions with developmentally delayed than with non-delayed children; and, as the children got older this difference increased, since mothers tended to use even more controlling questions with children with developmental delays and fewer with non-delayed children. Another study by Hanzlik (1990), of infants with cerebral palsy and developmental delay, also found that mothers of these infants were more directive and less positive in their interactions than mothers of non-disabled infants.

Mahoney and Robenalt, like Field, think that it is likely that this increased use of commands by mothers of disabled children results from their attempts to elicit a greater amount of activity from their child by asking them to do things; but that this could well result in the child becoming even less active.

Bray (1988) compared children with Down's Syndrome and severe learning difficulties aged between two and six years with two groups of non-disabled children (same chronological age and same mental age). She found that the children with Down's syndrome were less likely to be involved in interactions where they took the lead, or where the lead was equally shared between the partners, than children of the same chronological age. They were also less likely to experience equal interactions than children of the same mental age. Bray also found that the Down's Syndrome group were more likely to be involved in negative interactions and suggested that non-disabled children may stimulate their parents into appropriate forms of interaction whereas disabled children may not.

Although none of this research involves infants with PMLDs, there is some evidence that the more severely disabled an infant is the more acute these problems are likely to be. For example, Terdal *et al* (1976) and Cunningham *et al* (1981) found that children with more severe learning difficulties were less likely to respond adequately to mothers' initiations than those with less severe difficulties.

These research studies provide a good deal of evidence that parents and other caregivers find it more difficult to respond to children with disabilities than to non-disabled children, and are more likely to experience negative or unsatisfying interactions with them. Consequently infants with disabilities of all kinds are less likely to experience a responsive environment than non-disabled infants. Or perhaps we should say that they experience a less responsive environment than non-disabled infants.

Why not?

Why might this be? It could simply be because the adult knows that the infant has been labelled 'disabled' and responds accordingly; and in some cases this may contribute to the caregiver's problems. But if we return to our earlier example, we can see that for people with PMLDs the natural experience of a responsive environment may be difficult for a number of reasons.

For instance, hearing the voice of a familiar adult saying their name, the child with PMLDs may vocalise, like the non-disabled infant, but they might equally well relax slightly; a response not easily noticed and so less likely to lead the adult to continue interacting with them. Hearing the drinks being prepared, they might move their lips and tongue rather than smile. This movement might not so easily be connected with the drinks preparation, and so again might not be noted and commented on by the adult. Indeed, several investigators have noticed that both caregivers and staff such as teachers are less likely to respond to unconventional behaviours (such as tongue thrusts, eye blinks and shifts in position) as communication than they are to behaviours such as vocalizations (e.g. Downey and Seigel-Causey, 1988).

A child with PMLDs may not vocalize as frequently as a non-disabled child, and even if by doing so they attract the attention of an adult who responds, they may not respond to the adult's conversation attempt immediately, or in the way the adult expects and, consequently, the adult is discouraged from continuing the interaction, or even from responding to the child on a subsequent occasion.

When we examine interactions with the environment, the situation may be even more problematic. A child with PMLDs might be provided with a switch operated toy to compensate for the motor impairments which make it very difficult for them to work mobiles etc. They may move an arm, activating the switch and turn on the toy, which reacts with noises, lights and movement. Attempting to repeat the movement they may fail to activate the switch for several reasons: perhaps their movements are uncoordinated and they do not make contact with the switch pad, perhaps (due to the motor impairment) the effort of the first attempt has tired them, and they do not press hard enough, and so again the toy is not activated. Or there may be mechanical or electrical faults which again result in the toy failing to respond – another child may inadvertently have pulled out the leads, the batteries may be flat or the contacts dirty.

Research evidence backs the view that people with PMLDs do have some characteristics which make interacting with them more difficult and potentially less satisfying for the other person. For example they may 'behave' very slowly. Young infants have a natural behavioural rhythm – they do something for a few seconds (cooing, kicking their legs, etc) and then pause. Adults interact with them by waiting for the pause and then inserting a response, cooing back, talking to the infant, etc., and then pausing themselves, giving the infant an opportunity to respond again. In this way the basic turn-taking of conversation begins. A child with PMLDs may produce very few behaviours with very long pauses in between, so that it's difficult for the other person to get a feel for the rhythm; or there may indeed be little rhythm – a particular behaviour may at times be almost continuous with no pauses for an interacting partner to use.

Additionally it's possible that it is more difficult to tell what infants with PMLDs feel from the way they behave (their vocalizations, facial expressions and so on). We know from research on infants with a variety of disabilities, for example visual or hearing impairment, that the meaning of their behaviours may be difficult to interpret even for those who know them well (Dunst, 1985). Yoder (1987) demonstrated that for infants with learning difficulties and/or physical disabilities the difficulty in interpreting cues is greater for those with more severe disabilities. Again, this can make interacting quite unsatisfying or even stressful for the caregiver, who gets little positive feedback. Since this difficulty occurs for adults interacting both with infants who have sensory impairments and those who have learning difficulties or physical disabilities it seems very unlikely not to be the case for those who have a combination of some or all of these disabilities.

Wilcox *et al* (1990) examined the extent to which different adults (mothers, teachers, speech therapists) recognised communicative cues from children with developmental disabilities. They found that there were quite enormous differences between individuals; but over and above this they suggest that there may be factors specific to child-adult pairs which lead to some children receiving inconsistent responses to their communication attempts. Goldberg (1977) suggests that an infant's readability, responsiveness and predictability are all important in letting parents know that their behaviour is effective (and thus encouraging them to continue interacting).

An experiment by Murray and Trevarthen (1986) with non-disabled infants demonstrates just how important the infant's responses are in maintaining a satisfying interaction. Murray and Trevarthen asked mothers to talk to their infants via a video-link. When the conversation was 'live', mothers and infants responded to each other just as they would have done when interacting naturally. When mothers were played a recording of their infant but still believed they were in touch with them through the video link, they became conscious that the infant was not responding to them and their talk contained more commands and negatives. As Murray and Trevarthen point out, the mothers' behaviour in the recorded situation resembles that of caregivers in interaction with disabled infants. (Although the information obtained by this experiment is very interesting it is, to say the least, ethically dubious to obtain it by deceiving the mothers, as appears to have been the case.)

Perhaps though, this difference between the environment normally experienced by non-disabled young infants and that provided (both at home and at school) for those with PMLDs is an appropriate adaptation to their particular difficulties. Although a few writers suggest that this is indeed the case, the balance of the evidence from research is that the way adults (parents, caregivers, school staff) often adapt to people with PMLDs is not in the interests of their social and cognitive development.

Can we do anything about it?

If then a responsive environment is important to the development of social, communicative and cognitive skills, is there anything we can do to overcome the problems experienced in interacting with people with PMLDs in order to provide them with the type of interactive environment likely to facilitate their development?

In the next section we examine the evidence that it is possible to change interactive environments, looking at each of the three aspects in turn, and then go on to consider the implications for those who work with people with PMLDs. Not all the research addresses all aspects of a responsive environment, and much of it is concerned either with infants or children without any sort of disability, or, like that concerning differences in caregiver-infant interaction between disabled and non-disabled infants, with those whose disabilities are less severe than those this book is concerned with. Nevertheless it's this evidence which provides pointers to the sorts of investigation it would be useful to carry out with people with PMLDs, and it's also this type of evidence which underlies the research project on which this book is based.

Getting responses to one's actions

Anderson and Sawin's study with non-disabled infants (mentioned above) showed that it was possible to make mothers more responsive to their infants by means of a simple intervention procedure, and that this resulted in infants being more responsive, alert and positive.

McCollum (1984) worked with caregiver-infant pairs for whom social interaction had been identified as a problem area. She demonstrates that an individualized intervention, the Social Interaction Assessment and Intervention, enabled caregivers to adjust their interactions in the direction of greater responsiveness. The change in caregiver behaviour resulted not only in increased infant participation in the interaction, but also in greater enjoyment for both partners. This positive effect was true for infant-caregiver pairs with a wide variety of reasons for their social interaction difficulties, including at least one with severe cerebral palsy.

Barrera, Rosenbaum and Cunningham (1986) conducted a particularly interesting study with pre-term babies and their parents. Their study compared two forms of intervention, one aimed mainly at parent-infant interaction, and the other aimed primarily at the infants' cognitive development, and two non-intervention groups, one of pre-term and one of full-term infants. They found that both intervention groups made gains in cognitive development during the period of the study compared with the non-intervention group of pre-term infants, and that by the end of the study differences between the pre-term intervention groups and the full-term group had disappeared. Of particular interest is their finding that the group who had the parent-infant intervention most closely resembled the full-term group in the high levels of responsiveness of mothers to their infants, and in the extent to which they provided a variety of stimulation. Barrera *et al* suggest that the parent-infant intervention effectively 'normalises' the home environment. Like Bray (above) they suggest that, while normal healthy infants may stimulate their parents into providing experiences that foster development, the parents of infants with disabilities may need help to do so.

Opportunities to respond to the actions of others

Waiting for the child to respond is a critical feature of a responsive environment. Unfortunately because a child with PMLDs may respond very slowly, or not all, or in an unexpected way, there is a tendency for adults to behave as if they are not expecting a response. McDonald and Gillette (1984) say that caregivers and teachers are often surprised when they do wait for the child to take a turn, at what he or she is able to do. They also point out the need to wait in a way which suggests that a response is expected. In the Contingency-Sensitive Environments Project, we found that children were more likely to respond when the adult was looking attentively at the child while she waited.

Opportunities to take the lead in interactions

Turn-taking (waiting for the child to act first, imitating the child's behaviour, following the child's lead) was a major feature of an intervention used by Mahoney and Powell with parents and their moderately or severely disabled infants. They found that parents were, in general, very successful at implementing these strategies. Furthermore, implementation was associated with an increase in the responsiveness of the interactive environment the parents provided for their children, and with greater developmental gains for the children. However, for some parents there also seemed to be a negative effect in important areas such as warmth and enjoyment.

A study by Hauser-Cram (1993) which looked at interactive skills in general, found that the children of mothers who became much more skilled at interacting with their disabled children during the course of early intervention projects, made considerable progress in their cognitive and social development. One year into this study, it was not possible for the investigators to identify any differences between these mothers and their children and others for whom these large increases did not occur. They suggest this lack of difference between those who did and those who did not show major improvement is positive, suggesting that caregiver and child characteristics are not crucial factors in improving interactions. However there may have been important differences in delivery of the intervention to these mothers and children, which were not examined in this study.

Other important aspects of a responsive environment

The possibility of accelerating cognitive and social development is not however the only reason why we see it as important to provide a responsive environment for people with PMLDs. At the most fundamental level a responsive environment is important because it is through our interactions with others that we learn who we are. The educational philosopher Aspin argues that it is this principle which underlies the whole special educational enterprise (Aspin 1982). His argument is similar to that of the communication experts we examined earlier, that it is by being treated as communicators that we learn to communicate, but more comprehensive. He suggests that it is by interaction with other persons that we learn to become persons. It is not necessary to follow the philosophical logic involved in this argument to grasp the essential point that is being made, that interaction is important for personal development. As Aspin points out, this is at root a moral argument. In the end we are saying that it is important to provide people with PMLDs with a responsive environment, because experiencing this sort of interactive environment teaches us that we are valued and respected.

There is a third and more pragmatic reason why we see a responsive environment as important: that is its impact on staff who work with people with PMLDs. Classroom staff involved in the Contingency-Sensitive Environments Project reported increased enjoyment and satisfaction with their work. They generally put this down to their increased awareness of the children's responses. Like the caregivers of infants with disabilities, they found interactions with children who seemed not to respond positively stressful and unsatisfying; conversely they derived satisfaction and enjoyment from positive interactions with pupils.

The research reviewed in this chapter shows that there are subtle but important differences in the interactions with caregivers experienced by babies and infants with and without handicaps.

In summary: babies and infants with all kinds of disabilities and particularly those who have learning difficulties are likely to have interactions with their caregivers in which:

- they are rather passive partners;
- they get comparatively few responses from their caregivers;
- the caregiver is the dominant partner;
- there are clashes between the infant and the caregiver (ie both are 'speaking' at once).

Consequently, and very importantly, such interactions may well be less enjoyable for both infant and caregiver than those between a non-disabled infant and their caregiver. Although little of this research involves infants with PMLDs, there is every reason to believe that they will experience the same problems in interactions as those with less severe difficulties.

It is clear however, that a number of researchers have been successful in enabling caregivers (usually mothers) to alter their interactions in such a way as to create a more responsive environment for their infant, and that, in general, this has resulted not only in the infant themselves becoming more responsive, but in the interactions being more enjoyable and satisfying for the mother. There is also some evidence of a positive impact on cognitive and social development. However, all these studies (not surprisingly) have involved 1:1 interactions of an extended nature.

Most of the interactions experienced by pupils with PMLDs within a school context are not like this. For example, Goldbart (1980) and Ware (1987) both found that over 50 per cent of interactions in PMLD classes lasted less than one minute. Even where an adult is working with a pupil for a more extended period, it may well be that the main focus is not on the interaction itself, but on for example the completion of a physiotherapy or skills programme. Is it possible for staff to create a responsive environment under these conditions?

What little research there is on the interactions between adults and young children in groups suggests that it is more difficult for adults to maintain a responsive environment when they have responsibility for more than one child. For example Schaffer and Liddell (1984) found that nursery nurses were more likely to ignore children's initiations, and were more controlling when they were responsible for four children than in a 1:1 situation.

It seems, then, that if you are a member of staff involved with a *group* of people with PMLDs the odds are stacked against you in terms of having interactions with them that are responsive, and enjoyable and satisfying for you and them. Nonetheless, in the Contingency-Sensitive Environments Project we found that staff were able to create a responsive environment in their classrooms, without any increase in staff ratios, and without detriment to the activities they felt it was important for them to carry out with the children. The rest of this book is about how that was done.

CHAPTER 2

Getting started, making sense of children's behaviour

Introduction

The research which we reviewed in Chapter 1 suggests that the difficulties we may have in telling how a person feels from their facial expressions and behaviour (readability) and in engaging in turn-taking with them (synchronicity) when interacting with people with PMLDs may be at least partly responsible for the difficulty we often have in attributing meaning to their behaviour. Yet we know that we learn to communicate by being treated as communicators, and that it is being able to attribute meaning to our behaviour which enables others to treat us as communicators. If we are going to help people with PMLDs become communicators, therefore, it is vital that we learn to make sense of their behaviour.

Anyone who has worked or lived with an individual with PMLDs over a period of time probably already knows a great deal about their behaviour and what it means. However, we can sometimes be very unsure about how to interpret particular behaviours; and we may not always be aware of all the available information in making our judgements about their meaning.

As we mentioned in Chapter 1, there are a number of potential differences between the behaviour of someone with PMLDs and a young infant without disabilities which contribute to this problem. For example, someone may have a disability such as cerebral palsy which makes their movements jerky and uncoordinated, and therefore more difficult to interpret. They may very well take much longer than other people to make any response, and this can hinder our attempts to link their responses with particular events or lead us to conclude that they are not going to respond at all and perhaps abandon the interaction. They may have a severe visual impairment, and like young infants with such an impairment be unlikely to make eye-contact, making us unsure whether or not they are attending; or, as suggested by Fraiberg (1975) in relation to blind babies, they may move their hands when another child's response would be a change of facial expression. In addition, there are the other problems we have already discussed such as apparently continuous behaviour which allows you no space in which to respond.

Another problem, particularly with older people with PMLDs, may be the discrepancy between their level of functioning and their appearance. It's difficult (quite aside from issues of age appropriateness) to interact with someone who is physically a teenager in a manner comparable to that we would use with a newish baby, yet the young person with PMLDs may well be functioning at a similar level in many ways. This list of potential difficulties may seem very daunting; however, bearing them in mind may help us in our efforts to understand what an individual is 'saying' through their behaviour. Perhaps though, the greatest problem lies in the next step – using information about the meaning of behaviours to develop the communication skills of the individual.

Communicative intent

One approach which may be helpful in this regard is to look at the work on the development of intentional communication, of which there has been a good deal in recent years (See Goldbart, 1994, for a review). Although this development is actually continuous, many authors identify three important stages (See Table 2.1).

Stage 1

At first, the behaviours which adults use as signals of the baby's needs are involuntary responses to internal or external stimuli (for example startling to a loud noise, crying when hungry or screaming in pain). However, at a very early stage of development infants also engage in voluntary behaviour such as waving their arms and legs. Adults act as if the infant is trying to communicate through these behaviours; for example increased arm and leg activity may be interpreted as excitment about some impending event – 'Yes, we're going to the park very soon'.

1. Voluntary behaviour: e.g. arm movements, leg movements, apparently random vocalizations which do not seem to be connected to environmental events in any way, but are voluntary in the sense that they are under the individual's control rather than occurring as the result of, for example, a muscular spasm.
2. Purposeful behaviour: e.g. playing with a toy, walking deliberately towards something, picking up a piece of equipment.
3. Intentional communication: The child acts deliberately and spontaneously to affect someone else's behaviour: e.g. A child may reach out and touch you, look at you and smile or may initiate eye contact. They may vocalize when you have just left them to deal with someone else.

Table 2.1 Stages of development of intentional communication

Stage 2

Next, according to these researchers, the infant gradually begins to act purposefully, reaching out in order to pick up a toy, crawling across the room towards mum, or the sunlight streaming through the window.

Stage 3

Finally, the infant reaches the stage where they point to the toy out of reach on the shelf, and look at mum as if to say, 'Please get that for me'. This development is almost certainly assisted by adults interpreting purposeful behaviours as attempts to communicate, so that when a child reaches for a toy which is out of reach the adult intervenes saying, 'Oh, do you want me to get you the fire-engine?'.

This sequence, however, deals with only one aspect of communication, communication in order to achieve a goal. Much communication is not of this type, but is participated in for its own sake. In the Contingency-Sensitive Environments Project we identified another way in which behaviour develops from the first (voluntary behaviour) stage which we called 'Responses to the environment'. This includes behaviours such as looking up when someone passes nearby, or when the door squeaks or smiling and looking when the wind waves the leaves of a tree just outside the window. 'Responses to the environment' also include responses to other people who are not actually interacting with the individual concerned; such as vocalizing when another child/client vocalises, or in response to a particular member of staff speaking to another person.

Especially for pupils with profound motor impairments, who may rarely be able to demonstrate purposeful behaviour (at least without the aid of technology), this provides an alternative opportunity for adults to intervene in a way which will assist the development of communication. For example, when a child vocalises in response to the voice of a familiar visitor, the adult might say: 'Yes, that's Mary come to see us, do you want to talk to her?'

It is not really clear exactly where this type of behaviour fits into the sequence except that, like purposeful behaviour, it is nearer intentional communication than behaviour which is merely voluntary; but we could think of the sequence as being like that shown in Table 2.2.

1. Voluntary behaviour e.g. arm movements, leg movements, apparently random vocalizations which do not seem to be connected to environmental events in any way

2(a) Responses to the environment. e.g. Looks up when someone passes nearby, or when the door squeaks. Vocalizes when another child vocalizes, or in response to a particular member of staff speaking to another person. Smiles and looks when the wind waves the leaves of a tree just outside the window.	2(b) Purposeful behaviour. e.g. playing with a toy, walking deliberately towards something, picking up a piece of equipment.

3. Intentional communication. The child acts deliberately and spontaneously to attract someone else's attention, e.g. A child may reach out and touch you, look at you and smile or may initiate eye contact. They may vocalize when you have just left them to deal with someone else.

Table 2.2 Sequence of behaviours leading to communication

Of course, even when we include responses to the environment, this sequence doesn't cover all behaviours – since not all behaviours can appropriately be interpreted as having communicative significance. There are other voluntary behaviours such as eating and drinking, stereotypies, and also involuntary behaviours such as coughs and sneezes. As we will see in the next chapter, although these behaviours may not be directly concerned with communication they are important because they may provide either the occasion for communication or a barrier to it. In particular, involuntary behaviours are important because they attract a high rate of adult responses.

Additionally, whereas some voluntary behaviours can be usefully interpreted as communication, especially when they change following a significant event, others may simply be indulged in for their own sake. A specific example should help to make this distinction clear. Susannah, one of the pupils who took part in the Contingency-sensitive Environments Project, frequently moved her head as if looking around her. This behaviour, although voluntary, didn't normally seem to have any communicative significance. Sometimes, however, when a familiar adult came close to her, or when she heard another child vocalising, Susannah's head-moving increased and she might also smile and vocalise; this could appropriately be treated as an attempt to communicate, for example when Susannah responded to another child's vocalising by vocalising herself, an adult might say, 'Yes, Susannah. Isn't she noisy!'

One way, then, in which we can make sense of the behaviour of a person with PMLDs is to interpret it in relation to events which are happening in the environment. This is, in fact, very similar to what adults do spontaneously with young infants without disabilities; who learn how to communicate without the adult being particularly aware of the part their own behaviour is playing in the process. However, when someone has PMLDs, for all the reasons we've already mentioned, special efforts may be required to help them develop intentional communication.

The staff who took part in the Contingency-sensitive Environments Research Project found being able to think about individual children's behaviour in terms of the sequence given in Table 2.2 helped them in their attempts to use the potential meaning of behaviour to develop communication. In fact, in the Contingency-sensitive Environments Project we systematically examined the behaviours of each of the pupils in the classes involved in terms of the sequence given in Table 2.2. Discussion of each individual pupil used the form shown in Table 2.3 and focused around trying to place their various different behaviours within the sequence. The aim of this discussion (which took between ten minutes and half an hour for each pupil) was to give us an idea of both whereabouts in the sequence the majority of their behaviour fell, and what was currently their most sophisticated level of communication in the environment where we knew them.

The examples which follow show that, although it isn't always easy to sort out which behaviours an individual produces spontaneously, and which are responses to adult initiations, sharing views about the degree of communicative intent behind an individual's different behaviours can give everyone a deeper insight into the meaning these behaviours may have, and the type of environment which can help the individual to develop further.

Child:			Date: 00/00/00
	Behaviour	Context	Frequency
INTENTIONAL COMMUNICATION			
PURPOSEFUL BEHAVIOUR			
RESPONSES TO THE ENVIRONMENT			
VOLUNTARY BEHAVIOUR			

Table 2.3 Record form for individual pupil

> If you are coordinating a group working through the book together you will need to set aside some time (perhaps two half hours) to look at these examples and then hold a discussion about one of the pupils with whom you work.

Carol – A discussion about communicative intent

Carol was the first pupil we discussed during the Contingency-sensitive Environments Project, and the discussion about her is given in more detail here than are the subsequent examples, in order to demonstrate the process by which staff who work with an individual can build on each other's knowledge to both obtain a profile of the individual's communicative abilities and the environments which facilitate their use and develop their own expertise in making sense of the behaviour of people with PMLDs.

It became clear while we were talking about her, that people found it very difficult to identify behaviours which Carol engaged in spontaneously rather than as a response to another person. There seemed to be three reasons for this problem.

- First, most of her behaviours were in fact responses.
- Second, it was sometimes hard to decide whether a particular behaviour was spontaneous or a response to another person or to an event.
- Third, the staff who worked with Carol were accustomed to take the lead in interactions with her, and to looking for her responses to their actions, rather than to looking at what she was doing and following her lead.

This problem is not unique to Carol, or to the group of staff who worked with her, but is one which occurs frequently in environments for people with PMLDs, especially when education or training is involved (see for example the work by Houghton *et al* mentioned in Chapter 1). Those of us who are teachers, in particular, often see our role as instructing our pupils, and this tendency is exacerbated by the public view that pupils go to school to gain knowledge and skills. When this tendency is combined with the low level of spontaneous behaviour shown by many pupils with PMLDs it is easy for a vicious circle to develop in which the child learns that only responses are expected from them.

Thus, when we first started discussing Carol, someone suggested that her most sophisticated behaviour was sometimes smiling and making eye contact when an adult spoke to her. Of course, this was very clearly a response rather than a spontaneous behaviour, but knowing about it gave us an indication of the sort of spontaneous behaviours we might expect from Carol. Everyone was agreed that Carol only smiled in response to adult attention of some sort and never to attract attention or 'start a conversation'. Everyone was also agreed that Carol only sometimes smiled in response to an adult speaking to her. During the discussion it transpired that this was true not just of Carol's smiling, but of her other behaviours too, in fact several people thought of Carol as 'moody' for this reason.

As the smiling behaviour was a response we didn't try to discover whether there were consistent differences between the occasions when Carol smiled and those when she didn't, but if it had been a spontaneous behaviour, it would very probably have been useful to use some observations to find out. For instance, Carol may have smiled when some individuals spoke to her and not others, or she might only have smiled when the person speaking was standing very close and directly in her line of vision.

Establishing that Carol smiled only in response to someone speaking to her helped us to go on to find behaviours which she sometimes used spontaneously. Several people had noticed that Carol sometimes moved her head when things appeared in her line of vision – this was clearly a response to an environmental event; but there were two other things that she sometimes did which were possibly at a more sophisticated level than this. Carol occasionally vocalised; some people thought that she did this deliberately to attract attention, while others felt that she was probably responding to some environmental event such as hearing two familiar adults talking to each other, and still others wondered if it was simply a voluntary behaviour engaged in for its own sake.

Such disagreements between adults about whether a particular behaviour has communicative significance for an individual child are not unusual. For example, as was mentioned in Chapter 1, Wilcox *et al* (1990) found that for some children with developmental disabilities there was sometimes only a minimal level of agreement between three adults who knew the child well (mother, teacher and speech and language therapist) about whether they were communicating or not. Additionally they found that adults interpreted very varying amounts of behaviour as communication when interacting with different children, and appeared to be using different definitions of 'communication'.

However, while these disagreements are not unusual (and may be even more common when someone has very severe disabilities), they may mean that certain individuals receive very inconsistent feedback about the effects of their behaviour. Pooling views about the meanings of an individual's behaviour can help to ensure that they receive consistent feedback, even when we are genuinely uncertain as to whether or not a particular behaviour has a particular meaning, and this can facilitate the development of communication.

To return to our discussion about Carol; in addition to agreeing that she smiled or vocalised in some circumstances, several people had noticed that Carol sometimes lifted her arm when a familiar adult was talking to a nearby child; although people couldn't agree about whether this behaviour was intentionally communicative (i.e. that Carol was deliberately trying to attract the attention of the adult), everyone was agreed that it was specific to the nearby presence of someone she knew working with another child. It seemed, then, that this arm-lifting behaviour was the most promising with regard to developing Carol's communication skills.

An important point about this behaviour, is that it is not one which we would automatically and easily identify as being communicative – it isn't very readable. Additionally since it was both slow and silent, it could easily be missed by a busy adult who wasn't specifically looking out for it. So, although this arm-lifting seemed likely to be Carol's most sophisticated communicative behaviour (it was the only one everyone could agree only occurred in very specific circumstances), in terms of getting the sort of adult feedback which will help Carol to develop her communication skills the odds were stacked against her. However, once this arm-lifting behaviour had been identified as possibly intentionally communicative, people working near Carol could be on the lookout for it, ready to respond in an appropriate way. Additionally the chances of Carol getting a response to this behaviour could be increased by reviewing the way the classroom was organised (see Chapter 7).

As well as trying to ensure that everyone involved with Carol responded consistently to her arm-lifting, it would possibly have been useful to keep a record of the occasions when Carol vocalised. Vocal behaviour is the one which we most easily associate with communication, and is more easily noticed than many other behaviours; however, in our discussions, people were unable to agree how sophisticated Carol's vocalising was in terms of its communicative intent. Keeping a record could have highlighted any consistencies in Carol's vocalising and thus whether consistent responding to these vocalisations would provide an additional way of helping Carol to learn about communication. (See discussion about Jonathan on pages 23–25.)

Sanjeev – a discussion about voluntary behaviour

Sanjeev was a pupil with extremely complex needs and disabilities, including severe and poorly controlled epilepsy; and there was initially little agreement about the meaning of his behaviour. Some people suggested that Sanjeev responded to environmental events, whereas others were very sceptical about this, believing that these behaviours were involuntary – for example, Sanjeev would flinch if someone knocked his wheelchair or passed very close by. There was also disagreement about whether some of the other behaviours in Sanjeev's extremely limited repertoire were voluntary or not. For example, he sometimes seemed to smile; some people believed that these smiles represented minor epileptic seizures, while others felt that they were 'genuine'. However, people were eventually able to agree that some of Sanjeev's mouth and head movements were probably voluntary, and possibly changed in rate according to what was going on around him. Although they were at the least sophisticated level of communicative intent, these voluntary movements potentially provided an opening for the development of more sophisticated communication skills. For example, some people interpreted Sanjeev's head movements when sitting in his wheelchair as indicating discomfort; awareness that this might be the most likely explanation could lead to an agreement that when this behaviour was observed, staff would comment on Sanjeev's discomfort and offer to provide support so he could have his head up. This in turn might lead to the development of a 'conversation' where the adult also commented on the fact that Sanjeev was now more comfortable/could see better now etc. Additionally, responding to this behaviour in this consistent way would enable the hypothesis that Sanjeev's head movements indicated discomfort to be tested.

Sanjeev's mouth movements, which some people thought became more rapid when the classroom was busier, could be commented on as if that was true or as if they were in anticipation of some event. Thus even though, for Sanjeev, only very restricted voluntary behaviours could be identified, discussing these and their potential meaning offered the opportunity to provide an environment which would facilitate further development.

However, as Sanjeev's voluntary movements were very limited indeed, some staff felt that it would also be appropriate to try and develop his contingency-awareness (his awareness of his ability to affect his environment) through exploring the use of switches and microtechnology. Such methods have been found to be effective with people with very severe learning and physical disabilities by a number of researchers. (See for example the review by Glenn and O'Brien, 1994; and the recent book by Bozic and Murdoch, 1996).

Jonathan – responding to environmental events

Jonathan's voluntary behaviours, like Sanjeev's, consisted mainly of mouth and head movements; however he also occasionally vocalised. Discussion of Jonathan's behaviours highlighted the usefulness of supplementing such discussions with video and careful observation. Initially, almost everyone was unsure whether Jonathan's behaviours were purely voluntary or whether they occurred in response to environmental events. Examination of the video taken for the purposes of the project showed that Jonathan turned his head when an adult came to work near him, but out of his visual field. Additionally, the project team, with their privileged position as observers, had noticed that Jonathan's vocalisations were likely to occur when either another pupil vocalised or one particular member of staff spoke. Identifying these behaviours as responses to specific environmental events enabled staff to respond to them as if they were intentional communications, for example Flo, the member of staff to whose voice Jonathan vocalised, could make a variety of comments which treated Jonathan's behaviour as if it was an attempt to start up a conversation.

In all these examples discussion of the child's behaviours led to the identification of at least one voluntary behaviour which recurred with some degree of consistency in similar circumstances, and to which it was possible to attribute communicative significance. Except in the case of Carol's arm-lifting, there is no suggestion that the child intended to convey the meaning we gave the behaviour, rather that by responding as if the child had intended a meaning which is consistent with the

---

If you are coordinating a group you should pause here and begin your discussions about the people with whom you work. For the first time it's a good idea to chose someone who you're not sure really communicates intentionally, but whom everybody knows quite well – this will give everyone the chance to participate in the discussion. Use the form in Table 2.3 to help focus your discussions.

First give everyone the chance to say what they think is the most sophisticated behaviour the child in question shows. For each behaviour which is mentioned you need to find out:

- the situation(s) in which it occurs;
- how often people think it occurs;
- *whether it is a spontaneous behaviour or a response.*

When the group have identified one or more potentially communicative behaviours for the individual you've chosen to consider, think about ways in which you can alter the environment to facilitate the development of more sophisticated communication from these behaviours.

Before going on to consider other individuals in the same way it may be a good idea to read the section below on other ways of making sense of behaviour.

environmental events which probably cause it (or at least co-occur with it) we can help them to learn to intend. By repeatedly having his increased head-turning interpreted as a request to be able to 'watch', and receiving an appropriate response, Jonathan may learn that he is able to produce responses from other people, and come to act deliberately in order to produce those responses. Clearly one aspect of an environment which facilitates the development of intentional communication is the child's actions receiving consistent, interpretive responses.

Other ways of making sense of behaviour

The link between some of the behaviours described in the previous section and the environmental events to which they may be a response is very easy to miss in a busy classroom or a crowded shopping centre for example, and we may not even be convinced that this link exists (as in the case of Sanjeev increasing his rate of mouth movement when the level of activity in the classroom increases). In circumstances such as these it can be useful to carry out more structured observations of a particular individual's behaviour.

Such observations can either be based on an appropriate published assessment (see below) or on a home-made observation schedule. In Jonathan's case, for example, knowing that he sometimes vocalised, but not being sure if it was connected to a specific environmental event, we could use observation to check whether Jonathan, like many children, was vocalising in response to another person's voice. We might, for example, test whether Jonathan was responding to an adult's voice by setting up situations in which different members of staff were engaged in conversation and note any change in Jonathan's behaviour (see Table 2.4).

If, on the other hand, we wanted to establish whether Jonathan was vocalising when another child vocalised, we would need to use a recording system which captures the events happening around the time Jonathan vocalises. (See Table 2.5). The type of observation shown in Table 2.5 could, in fact, equally well be used to record whether Jonathan's vocalisations were related to adults speaking. An additional advantage of using structured observation to supplement the information we already have about a child's potentially communicative behaviours is that we can obtain a rough picture of the frequency of the behaviour we are interested in, which can be useful when we are deciding where to concentrate our efforts (see next chapter).

Most published communication assessments do not provide sufficient

Member(s) of staff involved in conversation	Type of Speech e.g. Normal conversation with another adult, speaking to another child, raised voices	Jonathan's reaction (if any)
(Extend columns as needed).		

Table 2.4 Record of Jonathan's reactions (if any) to adult speech

detail at the pre-intentional level of communication to be useful in developing communication skills at this early level. However, the Affective Communication Assessment (Coupe *et al*, 1988) can provide useful information to supplement that which can be gleaned from a discussion amongst people who know the individual well. The ACA consists of two sheets. The first is completed by presenting the child with a number of stimuli likely to elicit strong reactions; clusters of reactions can then be identified indicating things such as 'like' or 'reject'.

The second sheet is then completed to test out whether these reactions are general. Like the behaviours identified through discussion, information obtained through the ACA can provide the opportunity for

Children vocalising immediately previously	Types of vocalisation e.g. happy babbling, crying loud, prolonged	Observed by

Table 2.5 Record of vocalisations made by Jonathan

the child to learn that his or her behaviour can produce responses from other people. Goldbart (1994) also describes a more detailed assessment which she and a teacher colleague developed in order to identify pupils' strategies for starting, maintaining and restarting interactions (Goldbart and Rigby, 1989).

This may be a good point to mention the challenging behaviour which some people with severe and profound learning difficulties show. There is good evidence that for at least some people challenging behaviours develop as a result of less extreme communications not being understood, and that understanding the meaning these behaviours convey can help us to alter the environment in a way which enables them to convey the same meanings in less distressing ways. There are now a number of publications which can be helpful in examining challenging behaviour with its possible communicative significance in mind (e.g. Durand, 1990; Harris 1996).

If you are coordinating a group, you need to arrange times when you can discuss each of the people with whom you work in order to identify their potentially communicative behaviours and how the development of these behaviours can be facilitated. This probably seems a massive task – after all you may be working with five, six or even more people all of whom have their own idiosyncratic ways of conveying meaning. However, you will find that you can usefully continue such discussions as you read the next chapter, which deals in more detail with deciding which behaviours to concentrate on, and organising the classroom to provide a responsive environment.

In summary:

- We are likely to have problems in interpreting the behaviour of people with PMLDs, but being aware of the potential difficulties such as delayed and idiosyncratic responses can help us to be sensitive to the meaning of their behaviour. *But* those who know an individual with PMLDs well are often skilled in interpreting these behaviours.

- Thinking about the way in which communication develops in non-disabled infants (from involuntary reactions and simple voluntary behaviour through reactions to environmental events and purposeful behaviour to intentional communication) in relation to a particular individual can help us see the communicative potential in a wide variety of behaviours which are not yet intentional.

- Quite simple changes in the environment we provide can increase the chance of intentional communication developing from these pre-communicative behaviours.
- Useful supplementary information about the meaning of behaviour can be gained by using structured observation and published assessments designed for the purpose.

CHAPTER 3

Responding to People's Behaviour

In Chapter 1 we described a responsive environment as being composed of three parts: getting responses to your actions, getting the opportunity to respond to the actions of others, and having the opportunity to take the lead in interaction. This chapter deals in more detail with the first of these three aspects – getting responses to what you do.

We also mentioned in Chapter 1 that, in our initial investigations in classrooms for pupils with PMLDs, we found that the pupils had very few opportunities for interaction of any sort. In that research we also found that even those interactions which did take place were dominated by the adult, and that children received responses to only a very small proportion of their spontaneous behaviours. We found a similar situation at the start of the Contingency-sensitive Environments Project with the children receiving responses to only about 1 in 10 of all their behaviours. Of course, since there were always more children than adults in the classroom, many of the occasions when children didn't receive responses to their spontaneous behaviours were times when no-one was working specifically with them and levels of responses to behaviour which could easily be seen as communicative (such as vocalisations) were much higher. However, as we've already discussed, (see Chapter 2) even staff who know an individual with PMLDs very well may find it very hard to agree about when their behaviour should be regarded as communicative.

Additionally, even when staff were interacting with pupils, they dominated the interaction, taking the lead for about 90 per cent of the time. The issue of who takes the lead in interactions is dealt with in detail in Chapter 5 but it is also relevant in the context of responding to children's behaviours since an adult who is leading the interaction for a large percentage of the time is unlikely to be responding to the child's spontaneous behaviour even within the interaction.

Responding to children's initiations

Spontaneous behaviour, and responses to it, can occur either when the individual is initially alone, and their behaviour attracts the attention of someone else, who responds in some way, or in the context of an interaction which is already taking place.

Not surprisingly, perhaps, in the Contingency-sensitive Environments Project, when we examined staff responses to pupils' behaviours we found that even when a member of staff was working with an individual pupil, some pupils received many more responses than others. In fact, a complex picture emerged in which the extent to which staff responded to children's behaviours varied not only between individual children but according to the activity taking place, the adult involved in the interaction, and whether the child was initially alone or an interaction was already taking place. This is, you may remember, a very similar picture to that found by Wilcox *et al* (1990) when they examined interactions between different adults and developmentally delayed toddlers (See Chapter 1).

How many responses are enough?

The research on interactions between caregivers and infants which was discussed in Chapter 1 seems to imply that increased responding by caregivers to infants is always a good thing – regardless of the original level of responding. However, this needs to be seen in the light of repeated findings that infants with difficulties both do less, and receive fewer responses than those without difficulties. Indeed, some of these studies talk about the 'normalising' effect of their intervention on caregiver-infant interaction.

This raises some crucial questions. How many responses are enough? Or to put it another way, what proportion of behaviours need to receive responses in order to produce enhanced social and communication development? Is it desirable for a person with PMLDs to receive responses to 100 per cent of their behaviours, and even if it is desirable, is there some good enough level of responding which it is more feasible for staff to aim at? If 100 per cent responding is not desirable, what level is? Are different levels of responding desirable to behaviours which the individual produces when alone and those which s/he produces within an ongoing interaction?

The most fundamental of these questions is whether it is desirable for a person with PMLDs to receive responses to 100 per cent of their behaviours either during an interaction and/or when they are initially alone. There is little research evidence specifically on this issue.

Responding during ongoing interactions

However, with regard to responses during the course of an interaction, some insight can be derived from examining work on interactions between caregivers and infants without difficulties, even though this has dealt almost exclusively with situations where the caregiver is asked to engage the infant in interaction, and results are usually given in terms of the proportion of the caregiver's behaviours which were responses to the infant (see Chapter 5) rather than the proportion of infant behaviours which received responses. Exceptionally, Kaye and Charney (1981) do give figures for the extent to which mothers respond to different types of behaviour from their two year old infants during three play situations (with a tea-set, a picture book and a Fisher-Price play family) They found that mothers respond to over 80 per cent of all their child's behaviours (90 per cent of the time to those that seem to demand a response and 77 per cent of the time to all other behaviours). Although these infants were operating at a more advanced developmental level than most people with PMLDs, Kaye and Charney suggest that this picture mirrors that of earlier interactions. They argue that the adult takes the responsibility for keeping the interaction going even as the infant becomes more competent, and that progress occurs as the child gradually learns to take an equal share of responsibility for maintaining the interaction in successively more complex situations.

Responses to behaviours which occur when the individual is initially alone

Although there is no research on how caregivers respond to infants' behaviours outside the context of an ongoing interaction, investigators in other areas suggest that it is contingent responses which are important.

First, work on the development of contingency awareness using microtechnology demonstrates that it is important for the child to get feedback telling them that a particular action has caused a particular effect. For example Watson and Ramey (1972) conducted an experiment in which eight-week old babies were given daily sessions at home with a mobile which could be activated by pressure on a specially designed pillow. Fifteen of the eighteen children in their experimental group learned to work the mobile, as demonstrated by increased head movements. Several of the infants' mothers commented on their babies' enjoyment of the mobile, and one mother designed her own mobile which was worked by strings attached to the infant's feet. She gave the baby this 'home-made' mobile several times a day. Watson and Ramey found that not only did the infant activate his mobile less often after the 'home-made' version was introduced, but was observed to kick his legs vigorously when given the experimental mobile and then to become upset when it did not respond to his efforts. Glenn and O'Brien report a number of studies in which non-contingent stimulation before the contingency was presented (e.g. a mobile working independent of the infant's action) slowed or prevented learning. Additionally, Glenn and O'Brien found that developmentally young children were able to learn more quickly that a particular arm or leg movement produced an effect when an elastic band was provided for them to kick against in addition to the infra red beam which operated the computer controlled effect than when an infra red beam alone was used.

Secondly, theorists from a wide variety of perspectives see parental behaviour which is contingent on the infant's own behaviour as important for personality development. This view is supported by Breiner and Forehand (1982) who found evidence that young children who were developmentally delayed are more likely to receive undifferentiated positive responses to a wide variety of behaviours than children without difficulties. Similar results have also been found in relation to young children with Downs syndrome (e.g. Wishart, 1991) and it has been suggested that this lack of clearly differentiated feedback may have a negative effect on development of social interaction skills.

Additionally it may be helpful to ask what normally happens in everyday human relationships, the sort of relationships which we regard as fulfilling for ourselves and desirable for the people we work with. In everyday relationships we do not receive responses to every single action, and whether or not we receive a response depends on the meaning of our actions as perceived by the other person or people who are able to observe them. Consequently, identical actions may receive very different responses on different occasions. For example, if, during a coffee evening a friend observes me fidgeting, they might respond either by offering me a more comfortable seat (on the assumption that I am uncomfortable), or by trying to bring the evening to a close (on the assumption that I am bored), or they may not respond at all (because they see me as someone who often fidgets for no particular reason). In any of these instances their interpretation of my behaviour and their response to it, may or may not be appropriate. There are, of course, many occasions when, as adults we do not respond to each other's behaviour, because we do not regard it as requiring a response. This again highlights our predisposition to respond to the behaviour of others in terms of its meaning (how we interpret it) rather than its form (what the person is actually doing).

So then, for the great majority of people with PMLDs, an appropriate interactive environment is likely to be one where their behaviours are responded to discriminatively, with those behaviours which have most communicative potential receiving high levels of response, while behaviours which appear to be involuntary or engaged in purely for their own sake will receive much lower levels. However, like the environment experienced by a young infant, what is appropriate will change as the person changes.

How do different situations affect the responses of staff to people with PMLDs?

In our research we have found that staff in PMLD classes generally respond to between a quarter and a third of children's behaviours when an interaction is already taking place, a considerably lower proportion than that found by Kaye and Charney; although as we have already said this proportion varied from time to time according to a number of factors.

If receiving responses to what you do is important for developing communication and interactive skills therefore, and pupils with PMLDs generally receive a smaller proportion of responses than an infant functioning at a similar developmental level would from a caregiver, it may be helpful to compare situations where pupils with PMLDs generally received high levels and those where they receive low levels of response to their actions.

Personal factors

While it was clear that the main characteristic differentiating those children who received the lowest number of responses from their peers was that they tended to have fewer physical and more behavioural problems and to be unpopular with staff, the children who received the highest levels of response were a very mixed group, including both those from each school with the most profound learning difficulties and three physically attractive young children who were already communicating intentionally. In that to some extent these results mirror those of other researchers in a variety of environments for people with PMLDs and SLDs, these findings were not particularly unexpected. However, they highlight the need for strategies to ensure that those people least likely to receive responses to their actions do in fact do so.

Types of behaviour

In the Contingency-sensitive Environments Project we initially found that, whereas actions which were clearly or very probably intended to be communicative were responded to more often than other spontaneous behaviours, 'responses to the environment' were unlikely to receive responses from staff.

The behaviours to which staff responded most frequently, however, were involuntary behaviours – sneezes and coughs. Whether the child was already being interacted with or not, these behaviours attracted responses almost 100 per cent of the time. There are probably three reasons why this was so: first, coughs may be distressing and painful, and occasionally even life-threatening; second, in British culture it is usual to respond to coughs and sneezes, particularly when a child is involved. Third, these behaviours are usually very noticeable, involving loud noises and sometimes quite violent body movements. Although these involuntary behaviours have no communicative significance, the high level of response to them is positive in that it demonstrates that even in busy environments staff are able to respond contingently and consistently to particular behaviours.

In our previous research (where we classified children's behaviours not according to their level of communicative sophistication, but according to type) we found that vocal behaviours were significantly more likely to receive responses than non-vocal behaviours. Other researchers have also found that adults are more likely to respond to vocal than non-vocal behaviours. Taken together, these findings highlight the fact that the more you communicate, (or the more like communication your behaviour appears) the more likely others are to communicate with you. This further underlines the importance of being sensitive to the meaning of behaviours which would not normally be interpreted as communicative, and which may not be particularly prominent in a busy environment.

Activities

Children were also more likely to receive responses to their actions during some activities than others. Children's initiations during drinks received a higher than average level of response in both schools, as they did during physiotherapy in School 1. However, during language and individual work sessions (in School 2) children received a considerably lower than average level of responses to their initiations.

Although superficially these results may seem surprising, physiotherapy sessions in School 1 and drinks sessions in the two schools did have a number of factors in common. First, they involved a staff member working individually with one pupil at a time, and in close physical proximity to them – thus they were in a good position to observe any spontaneous behaviour engaged in by the pupil. Second, these activities involved repeated series of actions – the pupil is given a sip of drink, they swallow, they open their mouth, and are given another sip of drink. Within this context, one behaviour – the pupil opening their mouth – is clearly understood by the member of staff as an initiation on the part of the pupil – they want or are ready for 'more'. Finally, these activities were repeated on a regular daily basis, providing a framework which was familiar to both staff member and pupil, and within which pupil initiations were expected.

By contrast, in activities in which pupils received a low level of response to their actions, the staff member was often looking for specific responses from the pupil to her initiations. In language, for example, the staff member might be engaged in activities which were designed to elicit vocalisation from a particular pupil. Additionally, these activities took place on a regular basis and it might be that the pupils had learned that within these contexts they were not expected to initiate interactions. In other activities in which pupils received a lower than average level of response to their actions the adult might well be positioned to the pupil's rear or side, making it difficult for them to observe the pupil. For example, some physiotherapy sessions in School 2 involved the adult sitting with the pupil in their lap facing away from them.

Strategies for increasing your own responses

> If you are coordinating a group working through this book together you may want to read the whole of the section on strategies and decide which are most likely to be appropriate in your particular situation.

Staff who took part in the Contingency-sensitive Environments Project found two simple strategies helpful in responding more to children's behaviours: becoming aware of which pupils were receiving the lowest levels of response, and being aware of the potential for communication of behaviours which had previously seemed meaningless. Ways in which you can become aware of the potential meaning of behaviours which are otherwise difficult to interpret have been discussed in Chapter 2. Here we look at how you can become aware of which pupils/clients are receiving the lowest level of response and then go on to look at some other practical strategies for increasing your responses to what the pupil or client is doing, both when you are working specifically with them and when they are initially alone.

During the Contingency-sensitive Environments Research Project, feedback provided to staff included graphs demonstrating the amount and type of interaction being experienced by individual pupils. This feedback, combined with a greater awareness of the potential meaning of individuals' behaviours, enabled staff to respond more to those children who initially experienced particularly low levels of adult response to their actions. Thus, while at the beginning of the project some children received nine times as many responses as others; during the course of the intervention this difference decreased to six times, and in addition staff responded overall more to children's actions.

However, the type of feedback provided by the project staff was derived from detailed observations. Such observations are rarely practical except in a research context. However there are a number ways of making yourself more aware of the extent to which you respond to what different individuals do. The following exercise need take only a few minutes, and can provide you with feedback about your own behaviour, which, while it will not be as accurate as that obtained from detailed observations, can provide the basis for action.

Strategies which are particularly useful when the individual is initially alone

Exercise

Select two of the individuals from amongst those with whom you work regularly, preferably one with whom you find it easy to get on and one whom you find it more difficult to work with.

At the end of a period when you have been at least partly responsible for both individuals concerned, try to write down how many times you responded to something they did. What did the person do? Was it an entirely spontaneous behaviour or did it follow something you did? How did you respond? Compare your responses to the two individuals. Discount, for the purpose of this exercise, any occasions when they were responding to a request from you, and you simply praised their compliance.

> If you are coordinating a group, you may want to structure this exercise by ensuring that everyone has a few minutes to carry out the evaluation part at different times.

Responding to people you are not *currently working with*

Simply carrying out this exercise may well give you ideas about occasions when you could have responded to something that an individual did. But you may also be aware of a conflict between continuing with what you are doing with one individual and responding to another individual with whom you are not currently working. This problem is likely to become even clearer if you have the opportunity to take a video of an individual over a period of time when they are not being worked with individually.

In the Contingency-sensitive Environments Project we took five minutes of video of each pupil about every two weeks and then examined it for the events which illustrated various aspects of interaction. In one physiotherapy session the pupil we were filming, Elizabeth, had already received her physio for the day and was lying adjacent to a member of staff working with another pupil. On several occasions Elizabeth lifted her head and shoulders off the floor and looked and smiled towards the member of staff. This was unnoticed by the staff member who was concentrating on delivering physio and not facing towards her. Since this was a sophisticated initiation for Elizabeth, *and* was probably a deliberate attempt to start an interaction, when the staff saw the video they felt that they should take action to ensure that such initiations were responded to in the future.

One simple strategy for doing so would be to make sure that the member of staff closest to an individual not currently being worked with was facing in their direction (as well as attending to the person they were working with), see Figures 3.1, 3.2 and below, and had a clear idea of initiations to which it was particularly important to respond.

In Figure 3.1 Penny responds to Tracey although she is working with Darren. The photograph Figure 3.2 shows a group game (see Chapter 7 for further details). Penny has the children sitting in a circle so that they are encouraged to watch what others are doing and staff are able to see their responses. Here Darren is interested in what Penny and Ben are doing with a small ball which lights up and buzzes when warmed by a hand and Penny is positioned so that she is likely to notice his interest and respond.

To return to Elizabeth's attempt to attract attention by looking and smiling towards the member of staff working near her. Staff concerned with this particular example felt it should be possible for them to respond appropriately to initiations of this type even while working with another individual, as a comment addressed to her such as 'Are you watching so-and-so's exercises?' would be sufficient acknowledgement. However, not all people with PMLDs would know that they were being spoken to from

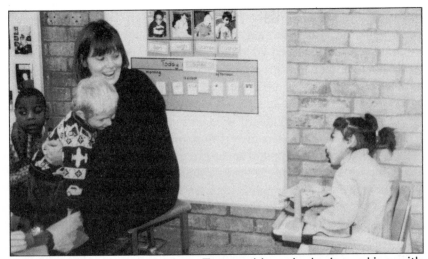

Figure 3.1 Penny responds to Tracey although she is working with Darren

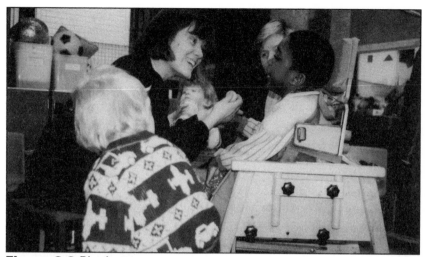

Figure 3.2 Playing a group game

a distance; or a greater level of response might be desirable. (for example it might have been appropriate to offer to help Elizabeth sit up 'so she could see better'). Other strategies for resolving the conflict may be required.

It is perhaps appropriate to add a word of caution about using video at this point. Easily used video cameras have revolutionised some aspects of observation and assessment. However, to be useful for this purpose video needs to be collected in a carefully structured way and watched with a clear idea of the type of events you are looking for. Even under these conditions it can be very time-consuming and disruptive. The suggestions about creating appropriate environments made in this book are deliberately designed to be useable without a large input of resources. If, however, you have the resources and are able to organise the videoing of individuals without undue disruption, we would suggest that you collect short extracts (say 5-10 minutes) at intervals in the day whatever activity happens to be going on, and then simply pick out the types of interactions you are particularly interested in. For example you might want to see which of an individual's behaviours have been interpreted as initiations and what responses they received.

If you are coordinating a group, and intend to use video you will need to remember that people can find watching video of themselves stressful, especially when other people are also watching, and it is worth laying down some simple ground rules for all those involved. Short extracts demonstrating exactly what you mean are a better use of time than watching the whole of a tape. Positive examples are much more effective than negative ones, and people involved should be clear that you will only be showing them engaged in the sort of interactions you are hoping to promote. You should also try and show examples of all members of staff interacting with clients in a positive way at different times. This means that to use video effectively you need to have the time available to watch each tape you collect and select appropriate examples from it. (Using video is discussed in more detail in Chapter 7 in relation to positive monitoring).

Organisational strategies

More highly structured organisational strategies may also be useful for increasing the extent to which individuals receive responses to behaviours they produce when they are alone.

Of course, in many organisations, for much of the time staff and clients or pupils will be involved in activities on an individual or small group basis. However, there are still some occasions when a group of staff is responsible for a larger group of clients or pupils, and research suggests that it is precisely in these sort of circumstances that individuals are most likely to have their initiations ignored.

Research has also shown that when groups of staff are responsible for large groups of clients or pupils with PMLDs, it is generally more effective (in terms of engagement in activities and the distribution of staff time amongst clients/pupils) for most staff members to have a particular role in relation to the whole pupil/client group than for them to have responsibility for a sub-group of clients/pupils. For example at a particular time one staff member may be responsible for assisting anyone who needs to use the toilet, while other members of staff may have responsibilities such as ensuring that everyone is engaged in an activity of their choice etc. One form of organisation which provides clear roles for staff is 'Room Management'[1] which has been extensively researched in environments for people with PMLDs (see Ware, 1994). Such systems are not primarily concerned with the interactive environment; however, within a framework such as 'Room Management' the likelihood of individuals having their initiations ignored can be counteracted by giving one staff member the role of being a 'responder' – responsible for responding consistently to initiations from clients/pupils who are not working individually with another member of staff. Of course it would also be possible to provide such a role within other forms of organisation.

---

[1] Materials explaining 'Room Management' and how to implement it can be obtained from the Mental Handicap in Wales Applied Research Unit

Strategies which are particularly useful during ongoing interactions

Organisational strategies can be of great help in clarifying the responsibilities of staff for ensuring that each individual within a group situation receives appropriate responses to their actions, especially when they are not engaged in specific individual or group work. However, there are many occasions when, as an individual member of staff, you may be working with one individual pupil/client in a wide range of situations – anything in fact from a shopping trip to an individual skill teaching session. Additionally over the course of a day or a week, you may work individually with a comparatively large number of people. In the Contingency-sensitive Environments Project, although staff successfully increased their responding to those pupils who were receiving fewest responses; even so, pupils received responses to less than 40 per cent of their spontaneous behaviours during ongoing interactions, compared with the >80 per cent of responses received by infants without difficulties from their mothers. Additional strategies are therefore required to ensure that individuals with PMLDs receive high rates of responses.

A number of investigators have remarked that one surprising fact about interactions between mothers and their infants with disabilities is that, although the infant produces fewer obviously meaningful behaviours than an infant without disabilities, the mother responds to just as high a proportion of these behaviours as do the mothers of infants without disabilities. Kaye and Charney suggest that, in the absence of meaningful behaviours, the mother takes any behaviour that the infant produces and attributes meaning to it. The behaviour may be treated either as a response to something the mother has said or done or as a new initiation on the part of the infant. A similar technique can be adopted during ongoing interactions with an individual with PMLDs. For example, if, during an art session, you have asked the individual with whom you are working to 'spread the blue paint' (with their fingers), and they do not respond, but a few seconds later they vocalise, you could respond to this either as a new topic of conversation – 'Oh you'd rather chat than paint would you, fair enough' or as a response to your request, 'You think it needs some more paint first? Right, here you are'. Of course it's important that such interpretations of behaviour are appropriate to the individual, for example that adults are addressed as adults.

Whether it is most appropriate to respond to all behaviours or selectively to those that are communicatively most sophisticated will depend on the individual's level of functioning. Looking at the behaviour of the people with whom you work in the way described in Chapter 2 provides a basis for deciding whether or not behaviours should be responded to selectively and, if so, which behaviours to respond to. However, where individuals have a range of behaviours at a particular level of communicative sophistication – whether, for example, this is simply a range of voluntary behaviours or a range of responses to the environment – some way of selecting those that provide the most useful focus for development is required. In this context, the following 'rules of thumb' are useful:

- Behaviours which can easily be developed into conventional communication – such as vocalisations which might develop into speech, or arm and hand movements which could develop into signs. (An additional reason for selecting vocalisations where possible is that research shows that they are more likely to attract responses).
- Behaviours which are easy to observe – these behaviours are more likely to attract a high rate of response in busy situations.
- Behaviours which occur fairly regularly so there are plenty of opportunities for responding to them.

Even if you working through this book as a member of a group who all work in the same situation, the prospect of trying to respond selectively to particular behaviours for each individual may seem overwhelming. A good strategy to adopt to ensure you don't become overwhelmed is to select one individual and try and respond consistently to one thing that they do. So, if for example, one of the people you work with regularly looks up when the door squeaks, you may (ideally after discussion with other relevant members of staff) decide to respond by telling her who has come in to the room, and sometimes asking additionally if she wants to say 'hello'. It's important to find a way of responding that feels natural to you, since you are trying to make this way of responding part of your normal repertoire of behaviours, and to keep the interactions between yourself and the people you work with natural and enjoyable.

If you are co-ordinating a group working through this book together, once you have discussed several of the people with PMLDs with whom you work in the way described in Chapter 2 you might suggest that each member of staff selects one person, and one of their potentially communicative behaviours to respond to, as a first step. People don't need to say which individual they've decided to concentrate on or all to respond in the same way. It's unlikely that several people will all select the same individual, since each member of staff will have their personal preferences amongst clients, and each person needs to respond in a way with which they are personally comfortable, if this way of working is going to become part of their normal behaviour.

Another strategy, which has been found useful in producing increased levels of responding both in interactions between caregivers and infants with difficulties and between staff and young adults with PMLDs, is simply to imitate the behaviour produced by the individual. Using this strategy can not only increase the level of responses the person gets to their behaviour, but also decrease the extent to which the more competent interactive partner dominates the interaction. The use of imitation will therefore be explained in detail in Chapter 5 which looks at enabling people with PMLDs to take the lead in interaction.

Summary

In this chapter we have outlined a number of personal and organisational strategies which can be used to increase the extent to which people with PMLDs get responses to their actions in group situations. Implementing organisational strategies needs the cooperation of everyone who works in a particular situation, but personal strategies can be implemented by one individual in a wide range of situations, although they are likely to be more effective if they are adopted by a whole staff team.

Organisational strategies

- Ensure that when an individual is not being specifically worked with, a member of staff who is working with someone else can see them, is aware of the ways in which they can respond, and the behaviours which it is particularly important to respond to.
- Use a roles system where a member of staff has responsibility for responding to those who are not currently specifically engaged in individual or group work.

Personal Strategies

- Whenever you are working with an individual, ensure that you are positioned so that you can observe any initiations they make and avoid being distracted by what other members of staff are doing or saying.
- Become aware of which people are receiving the lowest levels of response by monitoring your own behaviour.
- Become aware of the potential for communication of the behaviours in each individual's repertoire.
- Select behaviours to respond to on the basis of their communicative potential.
- Start small – select one individual and try and ensure you respond consistently to one thing that they do.

CHAPTER 4

Starting a conversation, giving the child a chance to reply

In the last two chapters we were concerned with developing ways of increasing our ability to interpret the behaviours of people with PMLDs and with increasing the extent to which we respond appropriately to those behaviours as attempts at communication. This chapter is about your attempts to start a conversation with someone with PMLDs and the opportunities they have within that conversation to respond to what you do – the second aspect of the interactive environment.

Why start a conversation?

Just as (as we saw in the last chapter) the context is important when we are responding to the behaviour of an individual with PMLDs, so it is when we are initiating the interaction. In particular, our aim or purpose in starting the interaction plays a large part in shaping the way it proceeds.

There are a number of different reasons for attempting to initiate an interaction with another person. We may, for example have a functional purpose in mind, getting assistance to move a heavy object, asking them to clear their things away, offering assistance with the washing up, helping them to get ready to go home, taking them to an activity in another room etc.

The 'conversation' may have a teaching purpose: for example, we may be demonstrating the way in which the lawnmower can be adjusted or we might be concerned with increasing an individual's skills and independence in preparing food and start an interaction with them focused on this task.

Alternatively, we may be starting a conversation purely for its own sake, as with any friend or colleague. In this case the topic of the conversation (whether it is yesterday evening's episode of 'Neighbours' or the implications of a 'leaked' government decision to impose VAT on children's clothes) may be less important than the pleasure we derive from the interaction. This example also illustrates another important reason why we engage in interactions with others, and that is because we believe that interactions are capable of influencing those who participate in them.

Of course an interaction often has more than one purpose. We may respond to a general appeal for help with the washing up both because we can see that there is a great deal to be done, *and* because we enjoy the company of the person requesting help. On one occasion the *outcome* of our discussion on motorway driving may be relatively unimportant compared with the pleasure of sparring with a close friend; on another we may be much more interested in convincing the other participant of our views than in the interaction itself.

Getting the child's attention

An interaction with someone with PMLDs may have any of these purposes (although research suggests that the majority of interactions between a member of staff and a person with PMLDs are of a functional nature; e.g. O'Connell, 1994). Conversations in differing contexts have different characteristics, different possibilities for development, and different pitfalls. However, particularly in relation to the actual start of the conversation, they also have things in common. Starting a conversation successfully involves checking in some way that the other person is ready and willing to participate, getting their attention, and signalling to them that it is a conversation we want and not a monologue. Most important of these is getting the other person's attention.

If we wish to start a conversation with a colleague who is working or reading on the other side of the room, we may go about this in one of several ways. For example we may monitor their behaviour, waiting for them to pause in their work, look up from their reading etc, before speaking. Alternatively we may say their name and then wait for them to look up, or give some other indication that we have their attention before continuing. In another situation we may wait until we can make eye contact with the other person before speaking. This is a strategy that we might well employ when there are several participants in the conversation rather than just two, or in a situation such as a check-out queue or canteen.

It can be useful, then, to think of the business of getting the other person's attention in order to start a conversation as being divided into two stages, first checking that their attention is available and then attracting and holding it. Any conversation, though, involves at least two participants. If the reader replies 'uh, huh' and continues with their book, or the person sitting opposite in the canteen looks away as we catch their eye, particularly if this is repeated when we make a second or third attempt, we may conclude that they are not willing to participate in a conversation at that moment. Often we employ strategies such as these for signalling our desire to participate in a conversation, or our unwillingness to do so, without really being aware of it. People with PMLDs are no different from anyone else in not always wanting to interact with us and if our attempts at interaction are going to be mutually satisfying we need to learn to read the ways in which they indicate that, just at the moment, they don't feel like being involved with us. We will return to this point in the next chapter.

Getting a word in edgeways – checking the availability of attention

The simple strategy of saying someone's name and then pausing is one we often use for getting the attention of someone when we need to interact with them for some functional purpose, such as asking them to get ready for a meal. If, for example, a child is absorbed in playing with their toys, or engrossed in watching television, we may call their name and pause before continuing, repeating this (perhaps with additional emphasis) if there is no response at first. Even this strategy, though, is more likely to be successful if we pick our moment for employing it with care, choosing a time when the other person does not have all their attention fully engaged elsewhere.

So picking the right moment to begin an interaction, or to be more accurate, picking an appropriate moment, is important in any interaction. But it is particularly important when the person with whom we wish to start our 'conversation' has PMLDs. Human beings have only a limited capacity for attention, and in general terms that capacity increases with increasing (developmental) maturity, as does the ability to divide attention between two simultaneous events. Someone with PMLDs, because they are developmentally very young, has both a much more limited capacity for attention and more difficulty in dividing their attention than an adult without difficulties. Secondly, impairments in the area of vision or hearing may make our efforts to attract their attention less obvious. Thirdly, because many people with PMLDs have experienced a rather impoverished environment, they may have become very absorbed in self-stimulatory behaviours.

However, just as we often employ signals which show whether or not we are ready to participate in a conversation, without really being aware of the process involved; we may equally be unaware of some the clues which tell us when we have a good chance of capturing another person's attention. Even if you are aware of these clues you may still have real difficulty in applying them to the people with PMLDs with whom you work, because their signals may be less clear than those of people who are already skilled interactors.

The examples which follow of successful attempts to capture the attention of people with PMLDs highlight the importance of careful observation in identifying times when attempts to begin an interaction are most likely to succeed, and the range of strategies which can be employed to make someone's attention available. You may also find these examples helpful in identifying the type of behaviours which may signal that an individual's attention is available to be 'caught'.

If you are a group coordinator, you will need to read through the examples before discussing them with the group. Be prepared to draw parallels between the examples given and particular individuals familiar to the group – this will both help the group see the relevance of the examples and facilitate the exercise given in the next box. For instance, you may have a client who, like Tanya, fusses when left or who sometimes seems to be listening to or watching events.

David – waiting for a pause in continuous behaviour

David is a five year old who can walk around, hold things, and coordinate his hands sufficiently to rub an object he is holding in one hand with the other. However, he rarely makes eye-contact, and appears to take no notice of most attempts to attract his attention. He has severe epilepsy with both occasional major seizures and frequent brief absences. His rubbing of toys is often accompanied by more or less continuous vocalisations of an uh-uh-uh type. Because he appeared not to respond when spoken to or to many other classroom noises, his teacher was concerned that David might be deaf. Joe, the peripatetic teacher for children with hearing impairments, observed David for some time and then sounded the bell he used to test young children's hearing. David immediately turned to the sound, and this demonstration was repeated on several occasions. Joe was thus able to establish that David had at least some hearing. By observing David acutely he had been able to pick an appropriate moment to try and attract David's attention, in fact he waited until David momentarily stopped both his uh-uh noise and his rubbing of the toy he was holding.

The strategy Joe employed to gain David's attention parallels that of waiting for the reader to look up from their book before speaking to them. Essentially, the observer waits for a pause, however brief, in the ongoing stream of behaviour and seizes it to get their 'word' in.

Clive – catching an alert moment

Clive was a pupil from one of the research project classes who had very profound learning difficulties and physical disabilities. He often seemed unwell and his breathing could be very difficult. Much of the time he was at school he spent either asleep or in a state which seemed somewhere between sleep and waking, showing little consciousness of the things going on around him. Often when he was timetabled for a particular activity he would be asleep. On one morning, he had slept through a language session, despite the best efforts of the member of staff to wake him and had continued to sleep as he was taken to another classroom for his mid-morning drink. As drinks began, and Clive's teacher, Penny, was starting to help two of the other pupils, Clive suddenly opened his eyes wide. Penny, seizing on the opportunity this offered turned to him and began a brief interaction.

Tanya – alert and 'listening'

Tanya, another pupil in the same class, had a much wider range of behaviours than Clive and, although she had profound learning difficulties, was functioning on a more advanced developmental level. Tanya had good head control when she was in a supporting chair, and would lift her head so that she could see what was going on around her. She also had some arm and hand movements which were probably voluntary, and could grasp an object placed in her fingers. Staff described her as fussing if she didn't get their attention; she would often vocalise loudly when left, and sometimes when staff were interacting with other pupils nearby. In addition to 'fussing' Tanya had a posture which staff described as 'listening' in which she would sit quiet and alert with her head up. Staff correctly interpreted this posture as signalling that Tanya's attention was available to be 'caught' for an interaction.

On one occasion, for example, Penny noticed Tanya in her listening posture as she was finishing off a language session prior to moving the pupils to another activity. Penny turned to Tanya and began an interaction based on the activity change. Tanya responded with a slight smile as Penny began the interaction, and continued participating in the interaction with Penny for the next five minutes, fussing on several occasions when Penny had to leave her to deal with another pupil, but quieting immediately Penny spoke to her again.

With both Clive and Tanya, Penny used her knowledge of the individual to pick a moment when an interaction was likely to be successful because the child was in an alert state (described by staff in Tanya's case as 'listening') but not absorbed in an activity. Penny's ongoing monitoring of the behaviour of those pupils in her class who she was not currently working with individually enabled her to capitalise on their readiness for interaction.

At a more global level, particularly with those people who function at an extremely early developmental level, their overall state of alertness is important for successful interactions. A number of researchers working with young babies and their caregivers have demonstrated that the baby is most likely to respond to attempts to start a 'conversation' when they are alert but quiet.

Figure 4.1 p.52 shows Penny with a pupil in another group selecting an appropriate moment to interact. This is a good moment to start. Tracey arrives at school alert but quiet, so Penny greets her and begins an interaction.

Exercise

Make a list of the four or five individuals you work with most regularly and note beside each name the things that make getting their attention difficult, such as continuous behaviours or frequently being withdrawn into themselves, then note any behaviours or changes in behaviour which you think act as signals that a particular individual is ready to interact.

Ideally, then, when we want to gain the attention of someone with PMLDs, we would monitor their behaviour for some indication that their attention was available to be caught (even if only briefly) and then try and engage that attention, perhaps by saying their name and pausing. However, it is not always possible to wait until someone's attention is available before we try to interact with them, so we need strategies for making that attention available.

If you are coordinating a group working through this book together, suggest that group members observe each other's interactions with clients and note **positive** examples of interactions being started successfully through an appropriate moment being chosen for the initial approach. If your group members are to find this exercise a non-threatening and useful experience you will need to be particularly careful to ensure that all the examples given are positive.

One way of introducing the exercise would be to give one or two examples yourself, building on the parallels drawn between the people the group are working with and the examples given earlier.

This would also be a good point to remind the group of the benefits to be derived from their differential knowledge of and skill with different clients (see Chapter 2).

You will also need to prepare for the meeting where the group are to report their observations of each other by ensuring that you have noted at least one example of an interaction being started successfully by choosing an appropriate moment for each staff member in your group, so that you are able to ensure that everyone gets some positive feedback.

Excuse me! – Interrupting attention concentrated elsewhere

In our everyday interactions, we have a number of alternative strategies for obtaining another person's attention, when they are apparently absorbed in something else. For example we may cough, shuffle or clear our throat. All these actions, like saying someone's name, serve the function of interrupting their concentration, and making their attention available to be directed towards us, just as it is when they themselves

Figure 4.1 Penny choosing an appropriate moment to interact

have paused for a moment.

These strategies may not be effective with people with PMLDs for two reasons; they contain an element of social learning, and they may not be sufficiently salient. However, there are some simple strategies which can be useful for getting and holding the attention of someone with PMLDs, especially when we need to interact with them for some functional purpose, such as taking then to another room or helping them get ready to go home.

These strategies include exaggeration (which is parallel to the additional emphasis we may put on someone's name when our first attempt to attract their attention has failed), touching the individual we are addressing, getting eye contact (techniques which are also used in everyday interactions) and using a significant object. Findings from caregiver-infant interaction research suggest that exaggeration may be a particularly effective strategy for gaining the attention of someone who is operating at a very early developmental level. The example which follows shows staff using a combination of these techniques (with a particular emphasis on exaggeration) to gain the attention of a boy who spent much of his time engaged in stereotyped behaviour.

Tommy – interrupting stereotyped behaviour

Gaining the attention of someone who is engaged in stereotyped behaviour in order to begin an interaction can be particularly difficult.

Tommy, a boy in one of the project classes, spent much of his time absorbed in watching his own hand-flapping. However, the staff who worked with him regularly had become skilled in a range of appropriate ways of breaking into his self-absorption so that his attention was briefly available to be caught.

Richard, Tommy's teacher, wanting to engage him in a group 'good morning' song spoke and signed in a slow and exaggerated way, at the same time moving his face close to Tommy's. Using this method, Richard was successful in breaking Tommy's concentration on his hand-flapping. Tommy continued to attend to the singing for several minutes.

On another occasion, an assistant, Jean, needed Tommy's attention. First, she said his name and tapped him gently on the arm. When this was unsuccessful, like Richard, she spoke slowly in a louder than normal voice, and moved her face close to Tommy's. Tommy's self-absorption was broken for a split second, but Jean did not succeed in capturing his attention, so she moved to a position where she was directly in Tommy's line of vision and repeated her greeting. This time she was successful in starting an interaction; Tommy looked at her and smiled.

A few minutes later, Jean offered Tommy a drink, and when he apparently gave no response, she tapped the cup gently on the table moving it into Tommy's visual field as she did so. Tommy's attention was caught by this strategy, and Jean was able to offer him a choice of drinks.

This example shows that exaggeration can take a number of forms. Jean and Richard both slowed down their speech and moved their faces closer to Tommy's and Richard made unusually large signing movements. Both Jean and Richard also spoke slightly more loudly than usual, and they could also have made their voices more emphatic. These exaggerations both made Jean and Richard's attempts more salient, and therefore more likely to attract Tommy's attention *and* gave him more time to respond to them.

Figure 4.2 p.55 shows Penny attracting Ben's attention by touching his arm and using an exaggerated facial expression.

Other ways of increasing salience

Sometimes even exaggeration of the sort that Jean and Richard used successfully with Tommy is not sufficient to attract the attention of someone who is very self-absorbed. In such circumstances it can be useful to emphasise your own features using things such as face paints, or glitter. Figure 4.3a shows Penny successfully catching Katie's attention by putting a glittery decoration (which is being used as part of a group game) on her head. Although Katie is still holding the rattle in which she has been absorbed in this picture, her face shows that she is, at least momentarily, paying attention to Penny, in contrast to Figure 4.3b where she is totally self-absorbed.

A conversation, not a monologue

The opportunity for the other person to respond (which Richard and Jean gave Tommy by slowing down their speech) is a crucial aspect of an interaction which is a 'conversation' rather than a monologue, and also of a responsive environment.

When we began to examine the sort of environments which people with PMLDs experience, one of the first discoveries we made was that other people often spoke or acted as if someone with PMLDs was unlikely to respond to them. This was especially likely to happen when a member of staff had a functional purpose in initiating the interaction (such as moving the pupil concerned to a new position, getting them ready for lunch etc) but it also happened at other times, even during conversations of which the main purpose was the conversation itself.

Of course, this sort of interaction occurs, at least in part, because holding a conversation with someone with PMLDs is genuinely difficult. As in the interactions between caregivers and infants with difficulties described in Chapter 1, the exceptional slowness with which a person with PMLDs may respond, and the likelihood that they will not respond as consistently as someone without difficulties, leads to an expectation that they are unlikely to respond. The other participant in the conversation may then start to behave as if they are not expecting a response and to assume a more and more dominant role in the interaction. As a consequence, fewer and fewer opportunities are provided for the person with PMLDs to respond. A vicious circle is created in which lack of response from the person with PMLDs creates an expectation that no responses will be forthcoming, and few opportunities for responses are given.

Of course, making sure you have the other person's attention before continuing with the conversation, by using the strategies already described in this chapter is a big step on the way to giving them the opportunity to respond, because it is by a response of some sort that you

Figure 4.2 Catching Ben's attention

know that you have their attention. However, you also need to ensure that you continue to give them opportunities to respond as the interaction proceeds.

> If you are coordinating a group working through this book together you need to make sure that copies of the information you compiled about individuals when looking at communicative intent (Chapter 2) are available for your next meeting. You will probably find it useful to look over these for examples of the type of responses made by different individuals before the meeting; and to read through the next section so that you can help the group identify some of the less obvious responses which individuals may make.

Fortunately, there are several easy-to-use strategies for altering your behaviour in order to give a person with PMLDs more opportunities to respond.

The simplest way of indicating to someone else that it is now their turn to 'speak' is to pause in your own speech or actions. We do this naturally in conversations with people without difficulties. But, pausing within a conversation in order to allow the other person a turn doesn't simply consist of not speaking. As we come to the end of what we are saying we also concentrate our attention on the other person, looking at them, and probably making eye contact. We continue to look at them as they take their turn. In the same way, when we pause for a response in

Figure 4.3a Katie's momentary attention to Penny's 'hair'

our interaction with a person with PMLDs we need not just to stop but to concentrate our attention on them. We need also to remember that because, in general, a person with PMLDs is likely to take longer than average to respond we may have to pause for what seems like a long time, and this may feel very awkward especially at first.

An additional strategy which can help you to concentrate on the person with PMLDs while you are waiting for a response, is to know what sort of response you might get; whether a smile, a cessation in ongoing behaviour, vocalisation, eye contact etc. The information you compiled while working through Chapter 2 is likely to contain examples of the sort

Figure 4.3b Katie absorbed in repetitive rubbing of her toy

of responses which you can expect from the various individuals with whom you work.

However, it may also be useful to know some of the types of response that you are likely to get, especially if you are working with someone who you don't know particularly well. Smiles, vocalisations and eye contact are things that we would all easily recognise as responses, but the response of someone who is still at a very early level of development or who, for example has a severe visual impairment may be less obvious. For instance, one of the earliest responses to develop is a reduction in the person's overall level of behaviour. This is similar to the 'quieting' response of a young baby on being picked up by a familiar adult. If someone has a severe visual impairment, they may respond not with their face, but with their hands (Fraiberg, 1975; RNIB, 1995); so while it may often be sensible to concentrate your attention on someone's face when you are expecting a response, you need to be aware of the other ways in which particular individuals may respond.

In the Contingency-sensitive Environments Project we observed the extent to which staff paused to give pupils the opportunity to respond. We found that some pupils, mainly those with the most severe difficulties, got comparatively few opportunities to respond. Staff taking part in the project found that a useful way of learning to pause sufficiently for pupils to respond was to select one of these individuals who got the fewest opportunities and make a conscious effort to pause for a response during one particular activity. Using this method staff quickly increased the extent to which they gave all pupils the opportunity to respond. They found (as we have consistently found in our research), that when they did this the person with PMLDs participated in the interaction more frequently and this made them more satisfying to be with.

Exercise

Observing whether or not someone gives their conversational partner opportunities to respond is quite simple, you simply have to look for pauses in which they concentrate their attention on their partner, and conversely, for times when you would expect such pauses to occur in normal conversation and they do not. Whether you are reading this book as an individual or are part of a group working through it together, you may be able to organise a situation where you video some of your own interactions to watch later, by leaving a video camera running for part of the day. You don't need good pictures for this, and you don't need anyone to operate the camera, much of the video we used for the research project was collected by leaving the camera on a chair facing what we wanted to film, so any borrowed video camera which can be placed safely where it can 'see' at least part of the room where you will be working will do. If this is possible, look at a few minutes of video, concentrating on picking out occasions when you *did* pause to allow the person you were working with to respond, especially those occasions where it was particularly difficult to do so. (For example if you had to move one person in order to work with another or were in a hurry). These examples from video taken during the research project should help you to do this. They also show how all activities from the most mundane to the more exotic can be made into conversations.

Kim and Cliff: Chances to respond during an everyday activity

Kim has already told Clifford that he is going to have a drink, and that she is going to fetch a choice of beverages for him.

As she returns Cliff looks towards her.

She responds, 'I've got you one'.

Kim offers Cliff a choice of 'milk or orange'.

She speaks slowly and distinctly and moves the item she's talking about slightly.

This gives Cliff the opportunity to respond

Which he does, first by lifting his head slightly and then by looking at the juice.

Kim now wants Cliff to help in pouring the juice into the cup. She takes his hand and begins to move it towards the jug and only then tells him 'Except that you have to help pour it. Hold the handle'.

(He doesn't really get a chance to respond)

He pulls away slightly.

Kim tells Cliff 'Look at what we're doing'.

Again he gets a chance to respond

And does so appropriately

It is noticeable from this sequence that Kim uses some of the same techniques for attracting Cliff's attention which Jean and Richard used with Tommy.

Linda and Mary: Giving opportunities to respond to someone with very severe difficulties

Linda is making bread with Mary.

Linda pushes Mary's hands onto the dough repeating in a sing-song voice 'Mary press the dough'. **She pauses** but there is no response from Mary.

Linda stops again and says 'Mary do it' and **pauses**.

Linda repeats 'Mary do it' and **pauses again**.

Linda takes Mary's hands and demonstrates.

Linda sings 'Mary press the dough' as she herself is banging it. **She pauses again**.

Linda demonstrates with Mary's hands again and says 'Oh it's lovely and warm'. **She pauses again** but still there is no response from Mary.

Linda rolls up the dough and says 'Shall we have another go?' Mary looks briefly at Linda (in response?) and Linda looks closely into her face.

Linda presses Mary's hands gently in the dough again and **pauses**. Mary looks at Linda.

Linda responds: 'Don't look at me' in a teasing voice.

In this interaction Linda persists over several minutes in pausing to give Mary chance to respond and eventually Mary does so. A situation in which the person you are working with does not noticeably respond despite repeated opportunities is one in which it is particularly difficult to continue to pause for responses. It would have been very easy for Linda to give up, and simply physically manipulate Mary's hands in the dough. Additionally, although Linda is asking Mary to 'press the dough', because that is what the activity demands, she is prepared to accept any response from Mary because she knows that Mary's repertoire of behaviours is very limited. In the next chapter we look at some of the strategies we can use to encourage a response in situations like this.

Ben: Looking for responses during physio sessions

Ben, like Mary, has very severe difficulties, and his ability to make physical responses is extremely limited. Like many people with PMLDs he needs regular physio/exercise sessions to ensure he retains as wide a range of movement as possible and doesn't experience unneccessary discomfort from contractures etc. Of course, many of the exercises the physio has prescribed for Ben involve passive movements, and it would be especially easy in this situation not to give Ben any opportunities to respond.

Figures 4.4a and 4.4b show how, although she carefully carries out the full range of exercises the physio believes Ben requires, Penny repeatedly gives Ben opportunities to respond, by doing the exercises slowly, pausing and keeping herself constantly in a position where she will observe any response Ben makes.

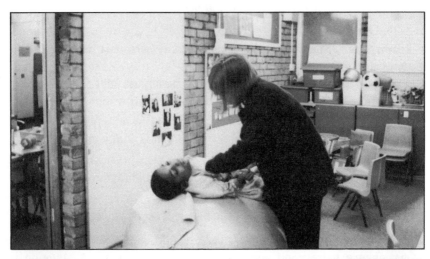

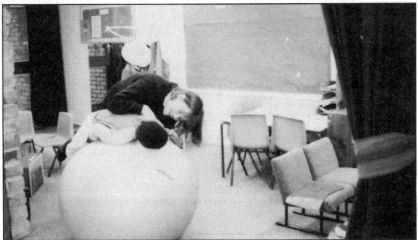

Figures 4.4a and 4.4b Penny pauses and watches for a response from Ben during a physio/exercise session

In summary: we can maximise our chances of being successful in initiating an interaction with an individual with PMLDs by:

- Being aware of the signals which indicate that an individual's attention is available.
- Having a variety of strategies for catching and holding their attention.
- Knowing what strategies may work when we need to interrupt an individual's attention to an activity in order to engage them in some other way.
- Signalling clearly that we wish to have a conversation with them especially by allowing sufficient pauses for them to respond and keeping our attention focused on their likely response.
- Giving them practice at 'conversations' by making sure that every activity (including those which are purely functional) provides opportunities for reciprocal interactions.

Being aware of when it is appropriate to end the interaction is also important and we need to be aware of signals the individual may use which show us that they have had enough for the time being, or that they wish the interaction to continue when we stop. These issues are dealt with in the next chapter.

CHAPTER 5

Sharing Control

The last two chapters have been concerned with specific aspects of interactions: responding in Chapter 3 and initiating in Chapter 4. In this chapter we look at the overall framework of the interaction. We examine both how you can keep a conversation going and how you can structure this to give the other person the opportunity to take the initiative, and thus to be an equal partner in the interaction. Finally we look at how we can know whether or not the other person wants the interaction to continue.

In Chapter 1 we described how, in both everyday conversations between friends, and in interactions between caregivers and infants, the participants take turns to speak or act and the lead in the interaction passes from one to the other. The opportunity to participate equally in interactions is vital for two reasons: it facilitates communicative and cognitive development, and it provides the opportunity for raising self-esteem.

Keeping the conversation going

In many of the conversations which we have observed between staff in various roles and the people with PMLDs with whom they work, however, the staff member frequently fills in the other person's turn and also takes the leading role virtually all the time.

For example when a pupil returns to school after the weekend in a new sweatshirt we might hear a conversation something like this:
'That's a nice sweatshirt Mary, it's new isn't it? I must say, red really suits you and is that a bird on it? Oh, I see it's an owl! – I bet you got it from your brother's club – Tim goes to young ornithologists doesn't he?'

Or like this:

'What did you do at the weekend Vijay? – Mum says you went to Southall market with Dad. And you got that new sweatshirt there. Did Dippi go too? No, I see, she stayed at home with mum.'

It's difficult to convey the feel of these 'conversations' in writing, without appearing to caricature them; because, of course, there's more to a conversation than words. But, in the first case, the member of staff is giving a running commentary on Mary's sweatshirt rather than talking to Mary about it. Mary is given little chance to join in, partly because the commentary proceeds without any real pauses; but also because, although superficially there are places where we might expect a response from Mary, in fact the commentary isn't really structured to allow her the opportunity to respond. You can get some idea of how this might feel from Mary's perspective by reading the commentary out loud, without really pausing for breath.

The second example is very similar, except that here the staff member supplies both sides of the conversation, rather than giving a running commentary; so that their monologue has the appearance of a conversation. The key issue is that, like the first example, the conversation isn't really structured to facilitate Vijay's responding. Again, you can get the idea by reading it aloud.

Of course, it's not surprising that conversations of this type take place, when we consider, that in terms of communicative competence, both Mary and Vijay may be functioning like young children, although physically they may be young adults. Indeed 'pseudo-dialogues' like these represent reasonable attempts by the staff member to keep the conversation going in difficult circumstances. Unfortunately, though, interactions of this sort aren't likely to help people with PMLDs to learn more sophisticated communication skills. So, how is it possible to interact with someone whose cognitive development may be very much at odds with their physical development in a way which encourages them to develop their communication skills?

When one of the participants in an interaction is much more competent than the other, it's natural for the more competent communicator to dominate the interaction, and when an adult interacts with a young baby, they initially control the structure and direction of the interaction. Infants without difficulties gradually come to assume a more equal role in interactions, because adults are skilled at enabling them to participate. In particular, as we discussed in Chapter 2,

64

caregivers attribute meaning to all sorts of behaviours which the baby does not intend as communications, accepting these as the baby's contributions to the interaction. Additionally, the caregiver structures their own conversational turn so that it is both a response to what the infant has just done and an invitation to the infant to make another response.

'Turnabouts'

Responses like this, consisting of a reaction to the other person's turn and a further invitation to them to take another turn in the conversation (called 'turnabouts'[1]) are characteristic, not just of caregivers' efforts to continue a conversation with a young baby, but of interactions between adults, and between adults and infants who are beginning to develop more sophisticated communication skills. Only when a number of attempts have received no response from the infant does the caregiver pretend that the infant has taken a turn or fill in their turn for them. However, when a child (or adult) has learning difficulties they are less likely to do something which the other person involved in the conversation can construe as a turn. How can we make it more likely that they will do so?

In the last chapter we talked about the importance of pausing with your attention on the other person, demonstrating that you are expecting a response, and being alert to any behaviour which can be interpreted as that response. In addition to pauses, the fact that we are expecting the other person to respond can be indicated by 'turnabouts'. However, these are comparatively rare in interactions in which one of the participants has severe or profound learning difficulties. The conversation with Mary includes two examples of responses from the staff member which could be turnabouts (italicized below), if they were followed by a pause to allow Mary the chance to respond, but only the second really qualifies, since the phrase which precedes the first cannot really be construed as a response to some action of Mary's.

'That's a nice sweatshirt Mary, it's new isn't it? *I must say, red really suits you* **and is that a bird on it?** *Oh, I see it's an owl!* – I bet you got it from your brother's club – **Tim goes to young ornithologists doesn't he?**

With sufficient pauses, the second part of the conversation with Mary about her new sweatshirt might have gone like this:

---

[1]The term 'Turnabout' was coined by Kaye and Charney (1981)

Staff Member	*Mary*
...and is that a bird	
on it? **Pause**	
	gurgles
Oh, I see it's an owl!	
– I bet you got it	
from your brother's club	
– Tim goes to young	
ornithologists doesn't he?	
Pause	
	smiles

Mary's turns in this conversation consist of very simple responses, but, nonetheless, the staff member's skill engages her in an interaction which has a conversational structure. This interaction is appropriate both developmentally (because its structure allows any response which Mary makes to be incorporated into the conversation) and chronologically (because a conversation about a new sweatshirt could take place with someone of any age).

By contrast, the conversation with Vijay contains no turnabouts, and, although, superficially, questions are being asked of him, in fact, the staff member responds for him.

If you are coordinating a group working through this book together, you will need to read through the examples of turnabouts given below and the exercise which follows well before the session in order to be able to give examples which are directly relevant to your situation.

The examples which follow illustrate staff from the project classes using turnabouts in a variety of situations to keep interactions going.

Chris and Nayake

Nayake and Dawn have been sat alongside each other by Paddy ready for Chris to work with them:

Chris says, 'Hello girls, are you all ready?' **Pause**
'Are you all ready and waiting?'

Nayake begins to smile and move her mouth.

Chris responds, 'Oh that's nice'.

Nayake smiles more broadly and begins to vocalise.

Chris responds: *'You were, were you? What did Paddy say? Did she say sit there and wait for Chris?'*

Nayake vocalises loudly, her face wreathed in smiles.

Chris says: 'She did, did she.'

In the italicised turnabout Chris acknowledges Nayake's smiling and vocalisation as if Nayake had told her what she had been doing, this facilitates the continuation of the conversation, and Nayake's next response is also incorporated as if she had confirmed Chris's statement.

Penny and Tanya

Penny has started Tanya's physiotherapy, and Elaine is shortly to take over to complete the exercises. The early exercises are ones which Tanya enjoys and she giggles constantly; but Penny then has to do some exercises which Tanya does not enjoy, and Tanya shouts in protest.

Tanya:	Shouts
Penny:	'Out and flat!'
Tanya:	Shouts
Penny:	*'Listen! I don't think that Elaine will want to deal with you.'*
Tanya:	Shouts
Penny:	'No she won't'
Tanya:	Laughs
Penny:	'No she possibly won't'.

The turnabout (italicised) enables Penny to treat Tanya's protesting as turns in the conversation; as a consequence Tanya stops protesting and joins in.

By treating the other person's action as a 'turn' in an ongoing conversation, turnabouts such as these enable a conversation to take place where otherwise there might have been no mutual interaction.

Exercise

Identify an individual who you interact with on a regular basis, perhaps someone who you take to a particular activity; and, in advance of the time when you will be working with them, identify the sort of responses that individual is likely to make. At the first opportunity write down the interactions which took place at the beginning and end of the session. (On this occasion it doesn't matter whether or not you can remember all the interaction accurately, the idea of this exercise is to help you become more aware of how you can respond to the people you work with in ways which promote interactions whose structure resembles a conversation.) Examine your responses and identify whether you used any turnabouts. Before your next session with this individual, identify ways in which using a turnabout would have enhanced the interaction and then repeat the exercise on the next occasion you work with this individual.

If you are coordinating a group working through this book together you may prefer people to observe each other's interactions to identify turnabouts. If you do, you will need to repeat the instructions about only making positive comments to others about their interactions which you gave for the exercise in Chapter 4. As in that exercise you will also need to have identified positive examples yourself for each member of the group. Alternatively, ask each staff member to identify when they wish to carry out this exercise and ensure that they have time immediately after their session to write down the interactions which took place.

Letting the other person take the lead

Turnabouts can be used to continue the conversation, not only after the other person has responded to your initiation, but in response to an initiation from them which may or may not be connected to the previous 'topic' of conversation.

Thus, when a caregiver speaks to a young infant, anything the infant does, from waving his or her arms to yawning, will be interpreted as a response. For instance, the yawn may get the response from the caregiver, 'Oh I'm boring you am I, well, what would *you* like to talk about?'

This type of response, of course, leaves the way open for the interaction to continue, since the next thing that the infant does can be interpreted by the caregiver as a new topic of conversation. In this way, not only is the interaction potentially continued, but the initiative is passed to the infant.

Often when we are talking to a friend or partner, perhaps trying to get a decision on what to eat for tea tonight, they are distracted, for example by something they remember they want to tell us or by an external event such as an unusual car passing outside the window. When this happens we may either follow their new train of thought before returning to the original topic, or try to get them to ignore the distraction. Sometimes an interaction will include many diversions of this sort.

Similarly when someone with PMLDs makes an initiation which is apparently unconnected with what you see as the purpose of the interaction it is possible to either follow their lead or try to continue with your original purpose. Obviously it isn't always appropriate to follow such diversions, but doing so has the advantage of handing over control of the interaction to the other person, even if only briefly.

Researchers trying to help caregivers of children with difficulties to be less dominant in interactions with them, have found that asking the caregiver to follow the child's interest helps to achieve this.

Sharing control is difficult for teachers but vital for children.

It is, perhaps, especially difficult to relax control if you are a teacher, whether by profession, or because your job definition includes teaching. There may be comparatively few occasions when you interact with your pupils/clients without having a particular purpose in mind. Often, we feel pressurised to achieve our goal and move on to the next task. Staff in other situations, too, will usually have a specific reason for interacting with the people with PMLDs for whom they are responsible, whether it is teaching a particular skill or initiating a leisure activity.

This contrasts with our interactions with our friends for which we often have no specific goal. Even with our work colleagues an interaction which begins for a particular purpose, for example arranging the time of a meeting, often changes into one which is less goal-oriented. Having agreed to the meeting, our colleague may well introduce an unrelated topic of discussion such as last night's television programmes, the cricket scores or the local news. Someone who has PMLDs may well lack many of the skills required for moving an interaction from a functional purpose to a pleasurable one. This means that those who work with them have to be especially alert to possibilities for allowing them to steer the direction of the interaction.

For example, Jill, a teacher in one of the project classes, was working with Ranvir trying to get her to grasp some bells which were suspended above her. Ranvir, however, was distracted by the patterns made by the sun shining through the window. Jill stopped, looked in the same direction as Ranvir and asked, 'What are you looking at? Is the sun making pretty patterns?' Thus, she implicitly acknowledges Ranvir's interest in the patterns and allowed it briefly to control the interaction.

In this interaction, Ranvir's interest in the patterns made by the sunshine is an unplanned event on which Jill capitalizes.

In a similar, unplanned way Beatrice (a teenager with profound learning difficulties but some simple intentional communication) in an interaction with Ruth (a nursery nurse) takes advantage of a pause which occurs while Ruth is recording to try and grab a piece of biscuit. Ruth laughs and asks: 'Are you after some more? – I think there's one more piece hiding somewhere – You have to sign for it.' Ruth has already helped Beatrice to sign biscuit, and Beatrice has already had some biscuit. Now Ruth responds to Beatrice's attempt to grab more biscuit, not with a reprimand, but as if it is a request for more. Thus, in a situation designed to teach a particular skill – signing biscuit – Ruth uses an unplanned event to enable Beatrice to take the lead.

Following the individual's interest can be made easier by providing materials in which we think they are likely to show an interest, either because they are similar to things which have attracted their interest in the past or because the materials themselves are likely to behave in novel ways.

As part of her 'tapping game' (described in detail in Chapter 6) Penny provided materials which she hoped would prove attractive to individual members of her group. Materials which attract interest in this way give opportunities to the staff involved to hand over control by following the response of the person with PMLDs as if it was an initiation commenting on or asking for the materials.

Other ways of relaxing control

Following the other person's lead is fine if they do something which either does provide a new focus to the conversation (as in Jill's interaction with Ranvir) or which you can interpret as providing a new focus. However, if someone rarely seems to do this, we need other ways of encouraging them to take the lead.

Pausing

In her interaction with Beatrice, Ruth capitalized on Beatrice's response to an unplanned pause (caused by Ruth's recording). In Chapter 4 we talked about the importance of pausing as a way of encouraging the other person to respond, but pausing can also be used as a way of encouraging the other person to take over the lead. For example, Richard in an interaction with Tommy, sets up a situation where the lead can easily pass to Tommy.

Richard has already made a chocolate spread sandwich with Tommy, most of which Tommy has eaten. Now Richard is looking closely at Tommy. He says 'Did you enjoy that chocolate spread sandwich?' and

pauses. A few seconds later, Tommy grabs one of the remaining pieces of sandwich and **Richard responds to him** 'Oh, he says so much so'. At this point the interaction moves to Tommy's control. Richard develops from Tommy's action, encouraging him to keep hold of the sandwich.

Waiting for the other person to start the interaction

Another important way of increasing the control experienced by the person with PMLDs is to give them the opportunity to begin the interaction. In Figure 5.1 Jenny, the music therapist, has come into the classroom to fetch one of the pupils for a regular session, but she waits without speaking, both for a pause in the ongoing activity which will increase the chances of whichever child she speaks to responding to her (see Chapter 4), and to see if anyone will initiate an interaction.

Figure 5.1 Jenny waits for Darren to finish putting names on the board

Imitation

In Chapter 3 we mentioned imitation as a strategy which can decrease the extent to which the more competent interactive partner dominates the interaction. When a caregiver interacts with a very young baby, one of the things they do naturally is to pick up on the baby's rhythm and insert their actions in the pauses between the baby's actions. If, in what they do, they also copy the baby's actions, this provides the baby with very positive feedback. This idea of imitating or echoing the other person's actions can be used deliberately with a person with PMLDs.

> If you are coordinating a group working through this book together arrange for pairs to observe each other and give feedback on *positive* aspects of interaction i.e. things which keep it going and allow the child to take over. Remember to stress the need to give *positive* feedback. It would be best to carry out this observation after people have had the opportunity to do the next exercise.

Exercise

Identify a time when you are likely to be interacting with a particular person. It can be any time, for example you may be responsible for helping them prepare for work, taking them to the toilet, assisting them in preparing the dinner or numerous other activities. If possible, chose someone who you know does not communicate intentionally (see Chapter 2). Once you have initiated the interaction try to hand over control to the other person, using one or more of the ways described in this chapter.

Miranda and Timmy

For example, when Miranda, a young assistant with no formal training other than that provided within the research project, is part way through a 'social skills' session with Timmy, she asks him: 'Are you going to have a biscuit again?' Timmy moves his head, putting it slightly on one side and Miranda imitates him. After this sequence has been repeated several times Timmy begins to chuckle.

In this example the imitation took place naturally within an ongoing interaction; but it is also possible to structure an interaction to include opportunities for the other person to do things which can be imitated. Imitation not only enables the other person to take the lead, it also often has the effect of slowing down the interaction, which also gives the other person more opportunity to participate.

Encouraging more equal interactions with peers

Of course, staff are not the only people who interact with pupils or clients, they also interact with each other. The Contingency-sensitive

Environments Research Project was not concerned with interactions with peers, but they are, nonetheless, important, for they can provide opportunities for people with PMLDs to be equal partners in the conversation.

Evidence from our own studies of integrated and segregated school settings (Ware *et al*, 1992) suggests (perhaps surprisingly) that children with SLDs initiate more during interactions with peers who also have learning difficulties. A recent study by Beckman *et al*, (1993) throws further light on these findings by showing that toddlers with mild to moderate developmental disabilities initiated interactions more frequently with a familiar peer (who didn't have learning difficulties) than with their mothers, even though, overall, they interacted for longer and in more complex ways with their mothers. Additionally, toddlers whose familiar playmate was closer to them in age initiated more than those with older playmates. Very importantly, mothers in this study were encouraged to select the playmate who they felt their child interacted with most frequently; who could well have been the child's own choice of 'friend'.

Most relevantly, Gleason (1990) describes the interactions between two young men with PMLDs, Danial and Thomas, on a 'total care' ward. The extract from Gleason's descriptions which follows is included to give the flavour of the reciprocal nature of the relationship between the two young men.

A key event occurred in the ward one afternoon during rest period when the teachers and professionals who were at lunch failed to return to conduct afternoon activities.

The first attendant passes by Thomas who is on the edge of the mat pushing a blue-handled Fisher-Price lawn mower into the aisle. She says to him, 'Now, Thomas, don't be pushing that out into the aisle.' She repeats herself more emphatically as she continues to walk by Thomas.

A second attendant finds the toy in the aisle and comments to the first attendant, 'they kill for this toy.'

Danial is brought in on a bed stretcher and laid down next to Thomas. Both boys are lying on their back. A foster-grandmother picks up a second lawn mower with a blue handle and places it between them. The Fischer-Price lawn mower has a wooden handle; one is white and the other is blue. The handle is attached to a plastic cylinder with coloured balls inside. When rolled across a surface, plastic wheels on either side of the cylinder turn plastic blades inside the cylinder. Coloured balls fly in all directions. The wheels engage a disk that repeats a tune over and over. When it rolls, the lawn mower displays popping coloured balls that seem to accompany the tune.

Danial swings the white-handled lawn mower over his head at a doll suspended from the ceiling. Holding it like a flag, Danial lifts the toy over his head.

An attendant sees the two boys together, picks up Thomas and says, 'Come on.' With another attendant, she brings him to another mat across the room. Hardly on the mat for a minute, Thomas starts to move across the floor.

In slow accordion-like movements, Thomas moves across the floor on his back half-inch by half-inch, a distance of twenty feet. Danial himself moves off the mat into the aisle maintaining his hold on the white-handled toy. Each boy stops his movement as the second attendant passes, glancing down and saying, 'This is their favourite toy. They all like it.'

In a series of three rolls, Danial finds himself head-to-toe with Thomas. Thomas manoeuvers himself into a position parallel to Danial. Each boy grips his toy and inches down toward the other, positioning the lawn mowers next to one another. Thomas reaches for Danial's white handled lawn mower. Danial pulls it back. He pushes the lawn mower forward as he moves back. Thomas grabs at Danial's white handle while Danial grabs at Thomas's blue handle. Suddenly, Thomas throws himself forward and grabs the white handled lawn mower. Danial seizes the opportunity to grab the blue handled lawn mower and raises it about his head. Thomas turns away from Danial and rolls the blue handled lawn mower on the floor.

The initiative in this interaction passes back and forth between Danial and Thomas and is clearly one between equal partners. It is also highly routinised and engaged in by Danial and Thomas because they enjoy interaction. Gleason comments that in this situation the two young men show greater interactive skill than in 'programmed activities designed for the purpose'. The level of complexity with which they interact is dependent both on the 'right partner' being present and apparently on the appropriate equipment.

As these examples show, encouraging peer interactions are another important way of increasing the opportunities that people with PMLDs get to take the lead in interactions, and assume a more equal share of control for the interaction. Observations which enable us to make and test out educated guesses about the meaning of an individual's behaviours in interaction with his or her peers are just as crucial as they are in enhancing the interactions between staff and people with PMLDs.

For people with PMLDs in integrated environments, access to opportunities to take the lead in interactions may be particularly difficult, since the probability is that peers, like staff, are more communicatively competent and tend to dominate interactions. Sometimes this is exacerbated, particularly in schools, by making a more competent individual a 'helper' to someone with very severe disabilities; it is easy for such role to promote interactions in which one person continually tells the other what to do and 'helps' them do it. However, we provide role models for the people with whom we work, and they tend to imitate our ways of interacting. If, then, staff give those people in the group with the most severe disabilities opportunities to be equal partners in interaction, this should 'rub off' on the others in the group.

The type of activities we ask people with more and less severe learning difficulties to do together are also important, instead of asking one person to help the other, you can provide activities in which both partners have an essential role or materials which are known to encourage interaction. (For example responsive toys such as those used by Cole *et al* in their studies, 1986).

'Push off!' or 'Don't go away yet' – being sensitive to the other person's wishes with regard to continuing the conversation

The final aspect of control relates to whether an interaction continues or ends. Often when we interact with someone with PMLDs we control both the start and end of the conversation; we have come to give them a drink and when the drink is finished we leave. But it may be that though we have finished, the other person wishes the interaction to continue. Alternatively, we try and continue an interaction when the other person wants to be alone.

If you have gone to see a colleague to arrange, for example, an exchange of shifts, as you are leaving the room, having completed the business, they say 'Oh, by the way...' This phrase and others like it act as signals that they wish the interaction to continue. Depending on the circumstances, you may pause and give them your attention or excuse yourself: 'Sorry Mary, got to rush...'

In the same way people with PMLDs may well have particular behaviours which they use as signals to indicate that they wish an interaction to continue. Although, just as with a work colleague, it isn't possible to continue the interaction whenever the other person wishes to, you can be alert to the strategies which individuals use to indicate their desire to continue an interaction and acknowledge their wishes even when you have to excuse yourself.

Tanya

Tanya, who was described in Chapter 4 as often vocalising when left by a member of staff who had been interacting with her, used this behaviour as a 'repair' strategy. On one occasion two members of staff, Penny and Elaine, were giving drinks to a group of pupils. As Tanya finishes the last mouthful of her drink, Elaine says: 'Let go then, good girl, all gone'. Having released the cup from Tanya's fingers Elaine moves away, and, having asked Penny who is to have a drink next she speaks to Clive: 'Right, would you like a cup of tea my love?'

Meanwhile, Tanya begins to move her hands and 'shouts'. Penny interprets this as a repair strategy, comes across to her, leans on the back of her chair, and says: 'Hey, listen here you, Elaine's just given you a drink. Don't deny it, she's just given you a drink.' As Penny leans forward Tanya makes eye contact. Penny then turns away to give a drink to Rosie, who is sitting next to Tanya. After being quiet for a short while, Tanya starts shouting again. Although Penny is occupied with giving Rosie her drink, she responds to Tanya again, saying: 'No, you've had a drink, you'll just have to wait a few minutes.' When Tanya continues shouting Penny briefly comes over to her and says 'You've had a drink, you h-a-v-e to w-a-i-t.' Tanya smiles. When Penny has to go to the other side of the room to attend to another child who is unwell, Tanya shouts louder and louder.

Clive

Clive, who was also mentioned in the last chapter, had very profound learning difficulties and physical disabilities. On one occasion when Penny was doing Clive's physio, she had to leave him briefly. While she was gone he began to move his mouth, and these movements appeared to diminish when she returned. It is not clear that these movements were intended as a repair strategy, they may have been a reaction to Penny no longer moving his limbs, but they could be treated as if they were intended to indicate that Clive wished the interaction to continue, particularly if they were observed on other occasions as a member of staff left him.

Tanya has clear strategies for attempting to repair interactions which have been broken off, and when she is initially unsuccessful she persists in her attempts. With Clive on the other hand, it is far less clear whether his behaviour when left is an attempt to repair the interaction.

If you are coordinating a group working through this book together you need to set aside some time in your group meetings to discuss the examples and begin to identify the strategies used by people with whom you work. For this exercise it is a good idea to start by looking at an individual who communicates in fairly clear ways. You may also need to make time for observations of those individuals whose strategies for repairing interactions are not known to the group.

This illustrates the importance of being aware of the strategies which individuals have for repairing interactions, so that you are in a position to respond. A first step in identifying these strategies would be to use a similar procedure to that detailed in Chapter 2 for initiations. However, for some individuals it may be necessary to use more structured methods, such as the observational assessment devised by Goldbart (1994). Obviously, it is often not possible to continue an interaction, but the individual's desire that it should can be acknowledged.

Exercise

Choose one of the individuals with whom you work (preferably someone who communicates fairly clearly) and identify the strategies they use to repair interactions. Next time you are working with that individual, plan time to respond to any repair strategies which are used as you leave. Repeat this exercise with an individual whose ways of communicating are less obvious.

Recognising when someone wants to end an interaction

When we are involved in a conversation which we wish to end, we all have strategies for escaping such as: 'Gosh is that the time? must dash!' or, less obviously, 'Right, I'll see to that'. If the other person involved seems oblivious to these social signals that we want the conversation to end we may get irritated (or alternatively desperate!) For example, we recently had a visitor who seemed just not to notice despite a succession of signals that on this occasion he had outstayed his welcome. After trying the more usual signals – 'Well it's been really nice seeing you...' 'We'll be in touch when we've had chance to talk it over...' I eventually got to my feet – a clear signal that I believed he was about to leave.

Such difficulties are comparatively rare in dealing with our work or leisure acquaintnaces. When we are interacting with someone with PMLDs however, we easily miss or ignore their signals that they have had enough of us for the time being. But allowing the other person to control when the interaction finishes is one way of showing our respect for them, and particularly important when the person cannot walk away. Additionally, being able to indicate that you want an interaction to finish is an essential part of learning to communicate.

One way in which some people indicate that they wish to finish an interaction is by turning away or avoiding eye contact. For example, Mary (who was mentioned in Chapter 4) sometimes turned her head away during an interaction. This happened at times which suggested that she might be trying to terminate the interaction, when she was bounced vigorously on someone's knee for some time, for example.

Another way in which someone may indicate that they wish an interaction to end is by the way in which they respond. They may respond less intensely or stop responding altogether. Instead of necessarily making our own initiations more intense when someone does this we need to consider whether they are trying to end the interaction.

Some people, of course, have more extreme ways of showing that they want an interaction to stop; for example Beatrice, who was mentioned earlier in this chapter, would try to push the other person away, and if this failed she screamed at them. Such extreme signals may sometimes develop when more low key indications have not been recognised.

Summary

In this chapter we have looked at ways in which our interactions with people with PMLDs can become more equal. Three aspects of sharing control of the interaction have been discussed.

- Keeping the conversation going by using initiations which are also responses to the other person's turn (turnabouts) and which enable us to accept any behaviour as a response.
- Enabling the other person take the lead by following their interest, and by careful use of pauses and imitation.
- Responding to the other person's desire to continue or end an interaction by being aware of their strategies for indicating this.

In addition we briefly indicated some ways in which equal interactions with peers can be encouraged. In the next chapter we examine ways in which people can be helped to become more competent communicators.

CHAPTER 6

Moving On

Making interaction more enjoyable for everyone concerned and teaching people that they are valued and respected as individuals are two very important reasons for creating a responsive environment; but at the same time, we want to help people with PMLDs to become more competent communicators and to develop both socially and cognitively. This chapter is concerned with how you can use the responsive environment to promote progress in these three areas.

If you have worked through the preceding chapters of this book and tried to apply the suggestions we have made in your everyday relationships with the people you work with, you may well already be aware of ways in which their communication skills are developing. In the Contingency-sensitive Environments Project we found that becoming aware of the meaning of people's behaviour meant that staff responded more frequently to intentionally communicative behaviours. Our observations showed that when the pupils received these higher levels of response they communicated intentionally more often. For example, Dorothy originally experienced very few responses indeed to her attempts to communicate; staff responded to her on average only 1 in 12 times. When examination of Dorothy's behaviour made staff aware of the probable meanings of her behaviour they dramatically increased the frequency with which they responded to her intentional communication, and Dorothy's intentional communications doubled. This suggests that simply being aware of how someone communicates is at least sometimes enough to change the pattern of interaction and begin a virtuous circle.

However, as you will be aware from your own experience in experimenting with the strategies suggested in previous chapters, responses from those you work with to changes in your behaviour designed to provide a more responsive environment are not always so dramatic. Indeed, it may sometimes be very difficult to discern whether there has been any change at all, particularly in people's spontaneous initiations. Yet, recognising such changes is important in adapting your own behaviour to facilitate further development.

One way in which such changes can be highlighted is by carrying out a reassessment of communication using the basic strategies described in Chapters 2 and 4. During the reassessment, behaviours identified previously as having communicative significance, being a response to an environmental event and so on are examined in order to see if their meaning has changed or become clearer, or if they have become more frequent or consistent. Secondly, any new behaviours, or new uses of previous voluntary behaviours are identified. Finally, ways of facilitating further communicative development are considered.

Child:	Date:		
	Behaviour	Context	Frequency
Intentional Communication	?Vocalisation	?To attract attention	Sometimes
	?Lifts her arm	?Trying to attract attention of nearby familiar adult	Infrequent
Purposeful Behaviour			
Responses to the Environment	Sometimes moves head	When objects appear in her line of vision	Sometimes
	?Vocalisation	?Hearing two familiar adults talking to each other	
	?Lifts her arm	When familiar adult working nearby	Infrequent
Voluntary Behaviour	?Vocalisation	Various	

Table 6.1 Recorded information about Carol

For example, the original discussion about Carol (see Chapter 2) revealed the information summarised in Table 6.1.

In addition, Carol was known to sometimes smile and make eye contact when an adult spoke to her; but no one knew why she sometimes responded in this way and sometimes didn't; indeed staff described her as moody. This description reflected our observations at the start of the project when Carol was responding to adults on average only one in three times. Examination of Carol's behaviour after the first period of staff training showed that she was responding more frequently (about one time in two), and everyone was now convinced that her arm-lifting was intentionally communicative; however, it was still very infrequent. Clearly a further increase in the frequency with which Carol responded was desirable and, as the strategy that staff had been using (which was to remember to allow Carol plenty of time to respond, and to observe her closely, so that any small response she made was not missed) seemed to be working, it was continued. Ten months later, after a further period of staff training, Carol was responding four out of five times. This was obvious to staff who reported that she was less moody. However, she still only very infrequently initiated an interaction, despite the fact that staff were managing to respond quite consistently to her very occasional arm lifting. In other words the staff's efforts in providing a highly responsive environment for Carol had only been partly successful.

How could Carol's communicative development be further facilitated? In particular how could she be encouraged to initiate interactions more frequently? There are several possibilities for building on the success which staff have already had in getting Carol to take her turn in an interaction when the staff member is taking the lead. First, since Carol is now responding consistently to adults, the technique used by Richard with Tommy in Chapter 5 could be adopted, with situations being set up where the control of the interaction could easily pass to Carol, possibly play situations which capitalize on her vocalising and smiling in response to an adult; or routines could be used (see below). Secondly, examination of Carol's responses to environmental events suggests that staff might decide to respond to these (turning her head when something comes into her visual field, and vocalising) as if they are intentional communications, as well as continuing to respond to her arm-lifting. Thirdly, staff could make special efforts to ensure that Carol had something to communicate about (see below).

If you are coordinating a group working through this book together, arrange to carry out a reassessment during one of your group meetings. (See exercise below.) Select an individual whose communication skills you originally examined three months or more ago.

Exercise

Reassess one of the people for whom you carried out an assessment in Chapter 2, concentrating initially on those behaviours which you originally decided to respond to *as if* they were intentional communications. Have any of them become more frequent? Do you now think that any of them are intentionally communicative? How do you know? For example, with a behaviour which you think is intended to attract attention, does it stop when you give the individual attention, and restart if you leave, as Tanya's did? (See Chapter 5). On the basis of this information, decide what strategies to adopt in order to help the individual concerned develop their communication skills further.

Using routines

Throughout this book we have drawn parallels between the ways in which you and other adults interact, and ways in which you interact with people who have profound and multiple learning difficulties. These parallels have been drawn, not simply in order to make the ideas we are trying to get across easy to follow, but because we believe that the basic structure of human interaction is the same regardless of whether a professor of philosophy is talking to a theologian about the existence of God, two children are excitedly discussing their proposed trip to Alton Towers, you are having an intimate conversation with a close friend, a teenager is helping her mother choose a new dress, a five year old is helping his big sister clear up, a toddler is sharing a picture book with her aunt, or a father is talking nonsense with his baby daughter. However, despite the common framework, there are important differences between these conversations in the extent to which the different partners take responsibility for the structure and continuance of the interaction.

In the first three examples it is likely that the two partners take equal responsibility, while in the last three one partner takes more responsibility than the other, ranging from the father who is more or less completely responsible for seeing that the conversation continues, to the big sister who can probably rely on her little brother to take about an equal share.

Within the framework of turn-taking, caregivers interacting with infants without disabilities seem naturally to adjust the way in which they interact as the infant develops, and this adjustment assists the infant's further development, as they are encouraged to take a greater share of the responsibility for the interaction. This adjustment is much harder with someone with profound and multiple learning difficulties for all the reasons mentioned in Chapter 1 (difficulties in picking up the rhythm of their behaviours, difficulties in 'reading' behaviour and expressions in order to know how they feel, conflicts between the expectations engendered by their appearance and the way they behave and expectations brought about by the 'label' which has been attached to them) and because, as we have already mentioned, the changes in behaviour which signal development may be so slow as to be almost imperceptible.

Routines

If someone, like Carol, responds to initiations only inconsistently, it is easy to repeatedly use any pattern of interaction which we know is likely to get a response. For example, if a particular individual almost always responds with smiles and chuckles to a game involving being bounced on someone's knee, and only rarely responds to other attempts at starting an interaction, we are likely to repeat the game again and again because it 'works'. There are some very positive features to familiar routines such as these: they provide a framework of turn-taking within which development is possible, and caregivers use them, not just with very young infants, but also with toddlers whose communication skills are developing. For example, the routine involved in playing a body-part game can develop from a simple one question, one answer situation (Where's your nose?) through a series of questions and answers (Where's your nose/eyes/ears?) and then showing parts on different bodies (Where's teddy's nose?) to a situation where the infant may point to a body-part and the caregiver supply the name, and finally to the infant naming the body-part concerned (Snow *et al*, 1982) as the child involved develops more sophisticated communication skills. There are simpler games than this such as 'Round and round the garden' which are also capable of development as the infant becomes familiar with them. In such games, the more competent communicative partner provides a number of slots for the other partner's responses; the numerous repetitions of the game (they may be played twenty or more times a day by caregivers and young infants) enables both partners to take their turns successfully.

Penny and Jill, two of the teachers in the project schools, had developed routines for use with small groups of their pupils. Penny's game consisted of tapping on, and looking in a box of assorted objects to select one. The children with whom Penny played this game were at varying stages of communicative development, and the game had a number of stages, as shown below.

Penny's tapping game : basic format

Penny:	*Timmy,* your turn to look in the box.
Timmy:	(hands on box)
Penny:	(taps and sings) Tap, tap ,tap, *Timmy, Timmy,* what's inside?
Penny:	(Turns box so opening is on top)
Timmy:	(hands in box)
Penny:	Oh, oh... *Timmy* look what's coming out!
	R-e-a-d-y
	It's a......

Although all that is initially expected as a response from the child in this game is to look, or respond in some other way as the object emerges from the box at the end, it was capable of a good deal of development and elaboration. Penny introduced pauses after 'look what's coming out' and 'ready' to allow any child who was ready for this step to look and anticipate the toy emerging. Eventually, the child could tap the box themselves, or initiate the game by reaching for the box, both of which we observed Timmy do.

In fact, although I have described this game for one child, Penny played it with a group, adjusting the way in which she played as she moved from child to child.

Figure 6.1a shows Penny playing this tapping game with a group. The routine begins with Penny sitting in front of a semi circle of children with the box, and singing her tapping song. Although this aspect of the routine is at a very sophisticated level compared with the current level of communication skills possessed by some of the children in the group, the regular repetition gives an opportunity for anticipation to develop, and individuals to respond to seeing the box in ways which can be treated as initiations. For example, one child might increase their level

Figure 6.1a Penny playing the tapping game with a group

of activity or vocalise more, and Penny could then respond by saying 'That's right, we're going to look in the box. Do you want first go?'

However, the children shown in Figure 6.1a have not yet developed this level of anticipation, so Penny selects Katie to start. The song is sung, and Katie is helped to pull out the Christmas decoration from the box. For Katie, Penny hopes at this stage merely to momentarily break her self absorption and achieve eye contact. Figure 6.1b shows she is successful on this occasion. As she becomes used to the routine, and in response to Penny's skill in selecting objects which attract her, Katie may reach out to grab one of them, and this can become the start of a

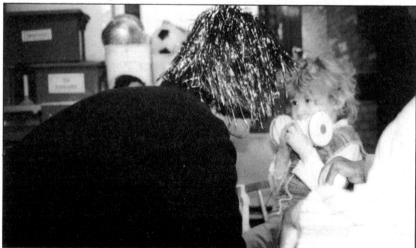

Figure 6.1b Achieving eye contact with Katie

Figure 6.1c Penny's interaction with Tracey

turn-taking routine with Penny.

As part of the routine of the game Penny now shows the object (Katie's choice) to the other members of the group. This provides further opportunities for anticipation, initiations, and mini turn-taking routines with individuals. For example, Figures 6.1c and d show part of Penny's interaction with Tracey using the decoration. Tracey shows great interest and even moves one hand towards Penny (Figure 6.1d), providing further opportunities for turn-taking.

With Darren, Penny tries to introduce a more sophisticated level of turn-taking by placing the object on his head, Figure 6.1e, and this

Figure 6.1d Tracey shows interest

Figure 6.1e Penny turn-taking with Darren

provides an opportunity for Ben's eye-tracking of the object (probably a response to the environment – see Chapter 2) to be treated as an initiation by Penny responding as if he has asked for a turn.

When it comes to Tracey's turn, after Penny has sung the song with the box held very near to her, Tracey (somewhat uncertainly), hits the box once – she is beginning to learn the routine, and take her part in it successfully.

Jill's game, which was a good morning song, incorporating pauses for the child to respond, was also played with a group. In both cases the fact that the game was played with a group, while it meant that each

Figure 6.1f Ben eye-tracking the object

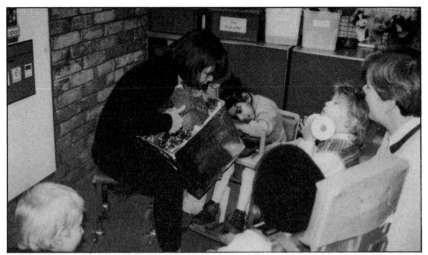

Figure 6.1g Tracey beginning to learn the routine

individual received fewer repetitions themselves, had the advantage of helping them to anticipate that their turn was coming by hearing the game played with others, and provided additional opportunities for initiations.

Routines such as Penny's tapping game have enormous potential for development, but it is also possible for routines to become 'fossilised' or sterile. The game may be repeated in an identical format time after time, with no space allowed for elaboration or the partner to take a more active part in it. Being aware of the ways in which caregivers and infants develop their routines as the infant becomes more competent can help in ensuring that the routines you use with the people with whom you work have the potential for development.

Exercise

Identify routines which you use on a regular basis with more than one individual, or a routine which you have used with one person over a period of time. In what ways does a particular routine change when you use it with different individuals? Has the routine you have used for some time changed over time? Is it possible to put these changes in order of complexity? Are any of your routines unchanging (and potentially fossilised)? Identify places where you could introduce developments, by writing out the routine in the format given (p.83) above for Penny's tapping game, and examining ways you could enable the other person more opportunities to respond or anticipate the next part of the routine (for example by leaving pauses).

One of the problems of trying to capitalize on the advantages of routines with older people with PMLDs is that those which come immediately to mind are likely to be games played by caregivers with young infants which are not age appropriate with older people. However, this does not have to be the case, routines can be part of reading a book together, and could even be introduced into tasks such as laying the table. Familiar tasks such as this in which both language and actions are highly predictable can provide the opportunity for gradually increasing participation and control in a similar way to a game routine.

Additionally, in our more intimate relationships, we often indulge in very familiar game-like routines even as adults. A couple may have routines in their private times together consisting of highly predictable turns. The group of young people walking across newly mown grass, and attempting to stuff it down each others' necks may well be repeating a routine. The family of parents and teenagers playing beach cricket quite possibly indulge in stylised rituals which have developed out of routines introduced when the children were much younger.

The groups of adult friends, as well as those of young teenagers, playing on the giant inflatables in the swimming pool near where I used to live, were often engaging in highly predictable routines. One person would climb onto the swaying inflatable, and as the inflatable rocked, (or was rocked by the other person) would fall off again into the water.

In these situations, the routines seem, as they are, a natural part of human friendship, and their predictability and repetitiveness is a valued part of the overall interaction. What may make such routines seem strange with adults with profound learning difficulties, is not that they are not age appropriate, but that, instead of developing 'naturally' they may need to be deliberately introduced and developed. However, there may also be times when we inadvertently impede routines which the people with whom we work are developing for themselves (see the example from Gleason's work in chapter 5). Becoming more aware of the meaning of people's behaviour also needs to be extended to their behaviour with peers, and particularly in making an extended assessment of someone's social interaction abilities, as Gleason suggests, observation of what they do with peers when we are not intervening can make a crucial contribution.

Other ways of facilitating the development of communication skills

Other aspects of the environment also need attention if people are to develop more sophisticated communication and social skills. One of the problems for people with PMLDs is that their lives may often be so impoverished that they have little to communicate about. By saying that their lives are impoverished what I mean is that they may be expected to use the same materials or visit the same places day in and day out, year in and year out.

Having something to talk about

Although, as we have said in earlier chapters, the content of a conversation is not always important – we may interact with our friends for the sheer pleasure of interacting; we also communicate enjoyable and novel experiences which have stimulated us to those who are important to us and, when we share such experiences, we converse about them. On a shopping trip we notice some unusual garment, 'Look at that coat! Can you imagine being seen in that?'. We visit a beautiful garden with a friend, and discovering a delicate flower hiding in a corner, we point it out to them: 'Look, at this, isn't that pink fantastic.' I am frequently laughed at by friends and family for the cry of 'Look, primroses!' or 'violets!' which I'm likely to come out with whenever we come across these flowers on a walk or a journey. But my pleasure at the unexpected appearance of splashes of colour on a motorway verge or in a hedgerow is an occasion for communication. If on foot, we may bend to examine the flowers more closely; 'Don't they smell gorgeous' or 'Look, this one's paler than all the others.' Even the small talk at a party suggests that it's easier to get a conversation going if we have something to talk about.

A friend of mine, who teaches a PMLD class, tells me that when he provides novel materials for his students, they behave in much the same way; examining the items and showing them to others. The novelty of the objects, and the opportunity to interact freely with them gives them something to communicate about, and they display their most sophisticated communication skills in this situation (Park: personal communication). The opportunity to handle things freely rather than just being shown them, is an essential part of this experience because of the early developmental level at which people with PMLDs are likely to be operating. Novel experiences of this type can be created in a number of fairly simple ways which do not involve using childish materials. To give just two examples: in a school situation, the artifacts which might be used as part of a geography or history session, if robust enough to be handled, could be put out for people to examine freely. The variety of things which are to be made into a collage can be put out for people to examine before use.

Staffing

One of the things which we noticed in the research project was that some children responded especially to particular members of staff. Perhaps the most striking example of this was Jonathan's response to Flo, which was mentioned in Chapter 2. Jonathan did not communicate intentionally, yet he appeared to recognise Flo's voice and respond to it as he did not respond to the voices of other adults. Discussion with Flo revealed that she and Jonathan had known each other for many years. Not only did Jonathan recognise Flo, but (not surprisingly) she was particularly skilled in interpreting his behaviour. This meant that Flo was potentially a key person in helping Jonathan to develop more sophisticated communication skills, not simply by responding when Jonathan vocalised at the sound of her voice (as suggested in Chapter 2) but also in other ways which capitalised on the special rapport between them.

In a busy environment involving a number of staff and pupils, ensuring that there were opportunities for Flo and Jonathan to enjoy turn-taking games together (for example) might well require special planning. However, given the difficulties in interpreting the behaviour of people with PMLDs and their problems in recognising unfamiliar individuals, the recognition of a particular rapport between an individual with PMLDs and a member of staff provides an important opportunity for mutually enjoyable interactions, and thus for the development of communication.

However, providing opportunities for people with PMLDs to spend time with members of staff they get on with particularly well, is not the only way in which the organisation of staff can facilitate their development. Both staff turnover, and movement of people with PMLDs between groups or classes can mean that the staff who interact most regularly with an individual with PMLDs change frequently. Additionally, both the sheer numbers of staff involved and the use of volunteers can mean that large numbers of unfamiliar people interact with a person PMLDs. For people who are operating at a very early level, it may be appropriate to limit the numbers of staff and volunteers who interact with them, as familiarity may well assist communication. For everyone, while meeting new people is important, organising staff so that there is always someone familiar around can help in ensuring that an individual's behaviour is understood and responded to.

Additionally, even simple routines such as playing a body parts game are carried out in different ways by different people, and different individuals will also have their own preferred routines. Join in a game of rounders with a number of families on the beach, and the first thing that has to be negotiated is exactly what the rules are. Often in environments for people with PMLDs we try to make roles which are fillable by a number of different staff. Of course this is necessary for smooth organisation, and has many advantages; but at the level of individual interactions, people are not interchangeable, and the different ways in which we do things are important parts of our personality. When someone with PMLDs is learning a new routine, therefore, it is probably best if it is carried out by the same staff member each time; as the routine becomes familiar, the natural variations in the way it is used by different staff members can provide new learning opportunities.

Cognitive progress

The evidence which was discussed in Chapter 1 suggests that the strategies which promote the development of communication will also facilitate cognitive progress. So recognising communicative development, and moving on in this area is likely also to encourage cognitive development. However, it can be just as hard, if not harder, to recognise progress in cognitive development as in communication. One of the problems is possibly the way in which we are currently encouraged to think about progress, which tends to devalue the achievements of people with PMLDs; and can also have a knock on effect on staff. Because this issue is vitally important to the question of how a responsive environment can be kept going on a long term basis, it will be discussed in the next chapter.

Summary

1. Being aware of the ways in which an individual communicates can mean that we respond more frequently to them and that this, in turn, encourages them to communicate more often.

2. It is sometimes very difficult to notice the progress that people with PMLDs are making; reassessment and knowledge of likely developments from their current behaviour can help us to become aware of changes in their behaviour.

3. The general framework of communication remains the same regardless of who is participating in the interaction, but the balance of responsibility between the partners alters according to their communication skills.

4. Routines which increase the likelihood of someone with PMLDs participating in the interaction can provide a useful framework for the development of communication but we need to be alert to the danger of them becoming 'fossilised'.

5. Organisation of staff and provision of novelty can also help in developing communication skills.

CHAPTER 7

Keeping the Responsive Environment Going

The last five chapters of this book have been concerned with how you can adjust the environment you provide for the people with PMLDs with whom you work in order to increase their opportunities to get responses to their actions, give responses to the actions of others and take the lead in interaction. The rationale for the this approach is, that by providing such opportunities, you will encourage interactions in which both partners participate more or less equally, even though it may well be that you, as the more competent partner, will be taking the lion's share of the responsibility for making this happen. We think interactions of this sort are valuable because they facilitate communicative, social and cognitive development, enhance self esteem and contribute to making your own role satisfying and enjoyable.

However, particularly if you are coordinating a group working through this book together, you may be wondering 'What next?' and, 'How do I make sure that I/we carry on interacting in positive ways?'

To some extent, a responsive environment may maintain itself. If, as you have adjusted the ways in which you interact, the people with whom you work have become more responsive and are developing communication skills, you will be getting some positive feedback about the impact of your efforts, and this will have made the job of providing them with a responsive environment somewhat easier.

But that may not be enough. After all, at least part of the reason why people with PMLDs often do not automatically experience a responsive environment is that they do not provide sufficient feedback to keep positive interactions going. When you are in a hurry, as you are likely to be quite often, it is hard to remember to keep giving opportunities to respond to someone who never seems to take them. Yet, a consistently responsive environment is particularly important for people who do not immediately respond to it, who may include those who have experienced years of living in an environment in which they have not been expected to participate. These people may need prolonged experience of responsive interactions if they are to learn that participating is worthwhile. In these circumstances we need to make special efforts to ensure that the responsive environment continues. In the remainder of this chapter we explore three strategies which can contribute to maintaining a responsive environment: increasing feedback, considering the activities we provide, and the way in which we provide them, and thinking about what we mean by progress.

Increasing feedback

If your interactions with those you work with do not provide you with sufficient feedback to ensure that you continue to interact in positive ways, the obvious solution is somehow to get feedback by some other means. One important part of the Contingency-sensitive Environments Research Project was that it provided the staff who took part with additional positive feedback. Both in group sessions and in individual meetings with staff, we were able to use our observations to demonstrate that their efforts to provide a responsive environment were being successful.

Jean and Tommy : drinks

For example, on one occasion at drinks time Tommy (who was sitting alone at a table) continued to pick up his mug and attempt to drink from it after it was empty.

As she approaches him, Jean calls out 'Tommy, would you like some more? Because that's empty'.

Tommy puts down his mug (which falls over) and turns towards her.

Jean rights the mug and looks closely at Tommy (who turns to her again). She asks, 'Would you like more to drink?' She then tries to wipe Tommy's mouth, but he pushes her away. Jean says, 'I know you don't like it'. She then moves slightly so she is looking directly into Tommy's face and repeats slightly more loudly, 'Would you like more to drink?'

Tommy again picks up his empty mug and attempts to drink. Jean says, 'Would you like more? Let's get the orange.' She reaches for the jug of squash and places it on the table. Tommy puts down his mug.

Jean again asks, 'Do you want more, Tommy?' He reaches for the jug and looks at it.

All the time Jean is observing Tommy closely.

Jean says, 'Good boy, hold the juice.' But as she puts her hand on the jug to help him pour, he removes his hand. Jean says, 'Hold it' and places his hand back on the jug handle saying, 'and pour it into your cup.' Tommy keeps his hand on the jug handle and continues to look as the squash is poured into his cup.'

As Tommy lifts his mug to drink, Jean removes the jug. Then she adjusts Tommy's table, commenting to herself in a low voice as she does so, and leaves Tommy to drink.

Discussion with Jean would start by asking her how she feels she is getting on with putting the responsive environment into practice. Feedback might then go something like this: 'I think you are responding more to the children's initiations. I really liked that time I saw you giving Tommy his drink the other day, I thought it was brilliant, you assuming that drinking from the empty cup like that meant he wanted more. You gave him lots of time to respond and he was really responding, looking at you and the jug, *and* putting his hand on it and that was really good for him.'

Getting feedback of this type is much easier if you are part of a group than if you are an individual working through this book alone. However, there are some strategies for ensuring that you receive positive feedback which are available to you even if you are working alone, or in an unsympathetic environment. The most obvious is to arrange to video some of your interactions (as suggested in Chapter 4) and then pick out examples (for instance of occasions when you gave the other person the opportunity to respond) which you feel particularly positively about. Although it is likely to feel strange, try and be specific with yourself about why you see the aspects of the interaction which you have selected as positive. For example, if Linda was reviewing her own interaction with Mary which was described in Chapter 4 she might feel especially positive about the repeated opportunities which she gave Mary to respond, when Mary seemed completely unresponsive. If videoing is not possible, you can still give yourself positive feedback, by 'rerunning' each interaction of the day in your mind and highlighting one positive aspect.

Exercise

Set aside twenty minutes at the end of your day or shift, and use it to monitor your interactions with those with whom you work. You may find it helpful to write out a list of those you interacted with, in order, and then beside each name write down one positive thing about the interaction. You may wish to do this with regard to one aspect of the contingency-sensitive environment at a time. For example you might look simply for occasions when you gave the other person the opportunity to respond to you. As you look for positive factors you will inevitably notice ways in which you could have improved the interaction as well. Try to see these in a positive light; noticing them gives you the opportunity to further develop your interactional skills. For Example: Mary – taking her to the toilet – having asked Mary to come to the toilet and turned her wheelchair to face the right direction, I gave her the opportunity to take over by waiting to see if she would wheel herself at all.

Try to carry out this exercise once a week or so, in order to keep the importance of the way in which you interact in mind.

If you are coordinating a group working through this book together and you have access to video equipment arrange to video one individual pupil/client at intervals over a week or so. These video sessions do not have to be very long, 5-10 minutes is ample; you may well be able to set up the video where it can 'see' the individual without the need for an operator. View the video yourself and select positive examples for use as feedback at a meeting of your group. This technique is particularly useful with individuals who have previously been identified by the group as receiving little positive interaction. Try and use a balance of two types of positive example; ones which demonstrate that responsive interactions are getting results; and ones that demonstrate members of staff being persistent even when they don't appear to be getting results.

You will need to have some time available for selecting the examples you wish to show, and to be particularly careful to avoid inadvertently showing parts of the tape where people are interacting in less positive ways.

Another way to use video for positive monitoring, but on an individual basis, is to pair members of staff and provide the opportunity for them to video each other interacting with a particular individual, and then watch the video together to give positive feedback. If at all possible let the pairs select themselves and make sure that you have emphasised the importance of positive feedback.

If you do not have video it may be that you are in a position to arrange for different members of staff to observe individual pupils/clients at intervals. For example, you might ask different members of staff to observe one particular individual at different times during the week noting occasions for example, when they were given opportunities to take the lead in interaction. As with video, individual observations do not need to be very long, ten minutes is ample. When these observations are discussed you will need to start by reminding people that feedback is to be positive. So, the observers could start by highlighting the times when they had seen a colleague giving an opportunity to take the lead in interaction. Only then would the group discuss how they could apply the techniques used to give the individual concerned more opportunities to take the lead. To end the discussion you would re-emphasise the positive examples and the range of strategies available to the group for giving the individual concerned opportunities to take the lead.

You could also adapt the exercise above, asking members of the group to run through their own interactions and those they have happened to observe and highlight positive examples which can then be shared.

Less formally, you can encourage members of the group to comment positively on each other's interactions.

It is important that these exercises are repeated at regular intervals if you are going to ensure that the responsive environment is maintained. Time constraints and other training priorities will almost inevitably mean that you can only carry out detailed video or other observations once every several months, but in the intervals in between, members of the group can carry out the exercise above for themselves with occasional opportunities to share positive feedback.

A responsive environment for staff

These ways of providing positive feedback to yourself and other members of the staff group may seem rather contrived or even cold. But noticing and appreciating the ways in which other members of your team interact with people with PMLDs and listening to their ideas and concerns is actually a way of showing them that, like the people with PMLDs with whom you work they are valued and respected as persons. Apart from the philosophical and moral arguments for this position, there is plenty of evidence to suggest that both being treated with esteem and consideration and being ignored and devalued rub off on those with whom we come into contact.

Planning activities

It has been our experience that where the main aim of an activity is the production of a particular thing, whether a Christmas cake, Mother's Day card, wooden tray or whatever, the interactions which take place between staff and people with PMLDs tend to offer little opportunity for participation by the person with PMLDs. In Chapter 3 we mentioned that in the research project we found a similar lack of opportunities for participation in activities, such as individual work, where a specific response is demanded of the person with PMLDs. Perhaps the problem with both these types of activities is with the way in which they are frequently focused: focusing on either a particular product or a particular response may mean that you become blinkered to other aspects of the interaction. If this is the case, then attention to the planning and organisation of these sorts of activities should help.

Whether you plan on paper, or simply by thinking about possible activities and ways of carrying them out, it is important to include a stage where you consider what responses you might expect to get from those people with the most severe difficulties. One individual may smile if they like the feel of something, and another withdraw their hand or turn away when they don't. One stage in the production of a Mother's Day card could be sticking tissue paper onto glued card. If while this operation is taking place someone responds by withdrawing their hand from the tissue, rather than pressing it onto the glue, having planned for the possibility of this response, you will be in a position to acknowledge its meaning. For instance you might comment, and then offer alternative materials.

If a product is involved, it is useful to think about what parts of the process are likely to be possible for each individual. For example, in her session making bread with Mary in Chapter 4, Linda concentrates on the process of kneading the dough. Although Mary has very profound learning difficulties, she does sometimes move her hands, and so it is possible that she will press the dough; and even if she doesn't, she may react to (and enjoy) its unaccustomed feel, and thus participate in the process.

So, we are not suggesting that people with PMLDs should not be participating in activities such as carpentry, cookery, gardening and so on. Indeed the novelty of some of the materials used in these activities may encourage them to communicate. Rather we are suggesting that activities such as these can be done in a way which is consistent with providing a highly responsive environment; by incorporating consideration at the planning stage of the ways in which the individuals involved are likely to respond.

One consequence for the staff in the project classes of providing a more responsive environment for their pupils was that they found activities taking longer than they had previously, and thus they were able to get through fewer things in the course of a day. This probably happened as the result of staff slowing down their interactions to give the pupils more time to participate. So another important feature of maintaining a responsive environment is to build some flexibility into the timing of activities. This may be very difficult, especially where each individual has a complex timetable of activities designed to meet their individual needs, but it is worth aiming for. There is little point in rushing from work experience to hydrotherapy, if you do not get the opportunity to participate in either.

> If you are coordinating a group working through this book together, arrange to collect information, in advance of individuals' reviews, about whether the organisation of their day allows sufficient time for them to participate fully in the various activities of which it is made up.

Progress

Caregivers of young infants get feedback partly from the baby's developing skills. The baby is interesting to be with, partly because with each passing day they are able to do more; the range of sounds they make increases, there is more variety in the way they respond to different people and so on.

In the previous chapters of this book, especially Chapter 2, we have emphasized the importance of increasing your own sensitivity to the meaning of people's behaviour for the development of interaction and communication; and if you have examined the behaviour of the people you work with in the ways we have suggested you have probably already become aware, not only of the meaning of some of their behaviours, but also of the ways in which their behaviour has changed over time. In working through the last chapter you may have been alerted to progress which you hadn't previously noticed. In saying this, we are not suggesting that you should have noticed this progress; rather that progress can be very difficult to spot. Being able to discover progress where previously you were unable to see it is important for maintaining a responsive environment, because being able to see that what you are doing is having a positive impact on the lives of the people you work with provides the feedback and encouragement we all need to keep us going.

Recognising progress has three important elements. We have already discussed two of these in relation to the development of communication; first, an increased sensitivity to changes in behaviour and second, knowledge of the normal course of development. The third factor which can contribute to recognising progress is to examine the way we think about progress.

In Chapter 6 we mentioned that the way we usually think about progress, which is in terms of progress towards predefined objectives, may not be particularly helpful in recognising the progress of people with PMLDs. When we talk about progress, we often do so in terms which imply that there is some absolute standard against which it can be judged. But just thinking about the everyday use of the word 'progress' suggests that this is far from true. For example, the recent addition of extra lanes to the M25 around Heathrow, and the proposed widening to seven lanes each way, is viewed by some people as progress, but by others as close to madness. Similarly, the protests over the Newbury bypass illustrate graphically the differences in view within one comparatively small community about what constitutes progress. The differing priorities of different groups and individuals lead them to have very different views as to what constitutes progress in all sorts of areas.

In the research project, in addition to observing the interactions of staff and pupils and offering training to the staff, we also talked to them about (among other things) their idea of progress as it related to children with PMLDs.

Several of the staff were very clear that many of those with no experience of people with PMLDs would come to the conclusion that they made no progress; but they were also clear that this was due to taking a rather narrow view of progress; and in a school context, stressing academic attainment, exam success or even self-help skills. As we have already suggested, it is not only educational views of progress (or success) which are problematic for people with PMLDs, but the general way in which our society thinks about it.

We are not suggesting that there is some new definition of progress which will solve the problem with regard to people with PMLDs. Rather, in the light of our discussions with the staff from the project classes, we have concluded that the most useful way to think about this issue is to be as flexible as possible.

At the very earliest developmental level for example, we might, as one of the teachers suggested to us, see as progress someone being awake for more of the day, or not crying all the time they are away from home, as settling more quickly after a holiday, or as reacting differently when they spend time away from their familiar surroundings, or taking their turn in a way that invites you to have another go, as well as in all the more usual ways.

This is not to say that the acquisition of new skills and of conventional ways of communicating is not important; there is no doubt that being able to communicate in ways anyone can understand is important; rather that even if we cannot discern any progress in these areas, there may well be other important ways in which progress is happening.

On this view, it is progress if someone who has been unhappy and upset is now happier and more settled. It is certainly progress if you are now able to tell when someone is saying that they prefer being helped by one person than another, even if that may be mainly because *you* have improved at interpreting the meaning of different facial expressions.

Summary

In summary: the responsive environment may not maintain itself; but it can be maintained by:

- Ensuring that staff receive positive feedback through positive monitoring.
- Positive monitoring can be carried out by observing yourself and others with or without the help of video.
- Planning activities to include responses which you know are possible for the individuals concerned and developing a wider view of what constitutes progress can also help to maintain a responsive environment.

Conclusion

In this book we have tried to show that a responsive environment is important for people with PMLDs, as it is for all people, because it facilitates the development of social awareness, communication and cognition, and makes life more enjoyable for staff. and above all because it demonstrates that people with PMLDs are respected and valued as individuals. We have also tried to demonstrate that such an environment can be created and maintained with the meagre resources for staff development and training usually available in settings for people with PMLDs.

References

Anderson, C.J. and Sawin, D. (1983) Enhancing responsiveness in mother-infant interaction. *Infant Behaviour and Development 6,* 361-368

Aspin P.N. (1982) Towards the concept of a human being as a basis of a philosophy of Special Education, *Education Review,* 34, 113-123

Barrera, M.E., Rosenbaum, P.L. and Cunningham, C.E. (1986) Early home intervention with low-birth-weight infants and their parents, *Child Development 57,* 20-33

Beckman P., Leiber, J. and Strong, B. (1993) Influence of social partner on interactions of toddlers with disabilities: Comparisons of interactions with mothers and familiar playmates. *American Journal on Mental Retardation 98* (3), 378-389

Bozic, N. and Murdoch, H. (1996) *Learning through Interaction: Technology and Children with Multiple Disabilities,* London: David Fulton

Bray, A. (1988) Social Interaction at Home of Young Children with Down's Syndrome. Paper presented at the 8th IASSMD Congress Dublin, August 1988

Breiner, J. and Forehand, R. (1982) Mother-child interactions: A comparison of a clinic-referred developmentally delayed group and two non-delayed groups. *Applied Research in Mental Retardation 3,* 175-183

Cole, D.A. (1986) Facilitating play in children's peer relationships: Are we having fun yet? *American Educational Research Journal 23*(2), 201-215

Coupe J., Barber M., and Murphy, G. (1988) Affective communication. In J. Coupe and J. Goldbart (Eds) *Communication Before Speech,* London: Croom Helm

Cunningham, C.E., Reuler, E., Blackwell. J. and Deck, J. (1981) Behavioural and Linguistic Development in the interactions of normal and retarded children with their mothers. *Child Development 52,* 62-70

Downing, J. and Seigel Causey, E. (1988) Enhancing the non-symbolic communicative behavior of children with multiple impairments. *Language, Speech and Hearing Services in Schools 19,* 338-348

Dunst, C.J. (1985) Communicative competence and deficits: effects on early social interactions. In E.T. McDonald and D.L. Gallagher (Eds) *Facilitating Social-Emotional Development in Multiply Handicapped Children.* Philadelphia: Home of the Merciful Saviour

Durand V. M. (1990) *Severe Behavior Problems: A Functional Communication Training Approach.* New York: Guilford Press

Field, T. (1983) High risk infants have 'less fun' during early interactions. *Topics in Early Childhood Special Education 3*(1), 77-87

Fraiberg, S. (1977) *Insights from the Blind: Comparative studies of blind and sighted infants.* New York: Basic Books

Garrad, K. (1986) Mothers' questions to delayed and non-delayed children, *Journal of*

Childhood Communication Disorders 9(2), 95-106

Gleason J. J. (1990) Meaning of play: Interpreting patterns of behavior of persons with severe developmental disabilities. *Anthropology and Education Quarterly 21*, 59-77

Glenn, S. and O'Brien Y. (1994) Microcomputers: Do they have a part to play in the education of children with PMLDs? In J. Ware (Ed) *Educating Children with Profound and Multiple Learning Difficulties*. London: David Fulton

Goldbart, J. (1980) Play Context and Language in the Special Classroom. Seminar Paper. Manchester, Hester Adrian Research Centre

Goldbart, J. (1994) Opening the communication curriculum to students with PMLDs. In J. Ware (Ed) *Educating Children with Profound and Multiple Learning Difficulties*. London: David Fulton

Goldbart, J. and Rigby J. (1989) Establishing Relationships with People with PMLDs. Paper presented to University of Manchester Dept. of Child and Adolescent Psychiatry Regional Study Day, 10th April 1989

Goldberg, S. (1977) Social competence in infancy: A model of parent-infant interaction. *Merrill Palmer Quarterly 23*, 163-177

Hanzlik, J. R. (1990) Non-verbal interaction patterns of mothers and their infants with cerebral palsy. *Education and Training in Mental Retardation 25*(4), 333-343

Hanzlik, J. R. and Stevenson, M. B. (1986) Interaction of mothers with their infants who are mentally retarded, retarded with cerebral palsy, or nonretarded. *American Journal of Mental Deficiency 90*, 513-520

Harris J., Cook, M. and Upton, G. (1996) *Pupils with Severe Learning Disabilities who Present Challenging Behaviour: A Whole School Approach to Assessment and Intervention*. Kidderminster: BILD

Hauser-Cram, P. (1993) Paper presented at the 60th Meeting of the Society of Research in Child Development, New Orleans Los Angeles. March 27th 1993

Houghton J., Bronicki, G. and Guess, D. (1987) Opportunities to express preferences and make choices among students with severe disabilities in classroom settings. *Journal of the Association for Persons with Severe Handicaps 12*, 18-27

Kaye, K. and Charney, R. (1981) How mothers maintain dialogue with two year olds. In D. Olson (Ed) *Social Foundations of Language and Thought*. New York and London: Norton Press

Lewis, M. and Coates, D.L. (1980) Mother-infant interactions and cognitive development in twelve-week-old infants. *Infant Behavior and Development 3*, 95-105

Mahoney, G. and Robenalt, K. (1986) A comparison of conversational patterns between mothers and their Down syndrome and normal infants. *Journal of the Division for Early Childhood 10(2)*, 172-180

McCollum, J.A. (1984) Social interaction between parents and babies: Validation of an intervention model. *Child: Care. Health and Development 10*, 301-315.

Macdonald, J.D. and Gillette, Y. (1984) Conversation engineering: A pragmatic approach to early social competence. *Seminars in Speech and Language 5(3)*, 171-183.

Murray, L. and Trevarthen, C. (1986) The infant's role in mother-infant communication. *Journal of Child Language 13*, 15-29

O'Connell, R. (1994) Proving integration works: How effective is the integration of students with PMLDs into the mainstream of an SLD school in increasing their opportunities for interaction? In J. Ware (Ed) *Educating Children with Profound and Multiple Learning Difficulties*. London: David Fulton

Paton, X. and Stirling, E. (1974) Frequency and type of dyadic nurse-patient verbal interactions in a mental subnormality hospital. *International Journal of Nursing Studies 11*, 135-145

RNIB (1995) *One of the Family: 1. First Sight. 2. Going my Way. 3. Making Contact. 4. That's What it's All About!*

Schaffer, H.R. and Liddell, C. (1984) Adult-child interaction under dyadic and polyadic conditions. *British Journal of Developmental Psychology* 2, 33-42

Scoville, R. (1984) Development of the intention to communicate: The eye of the beholder. In Feagens, L., Garvey, C. and Golinkoff, I.R. (Eds) *The Origins and Growth of Communication*. NJ: Ablex Publishing Corporation.

Shonkoff, J. P. et al (1992) Development and infants with disabilities and their families: implications for theory and service delivery. *Monographs of the Society for Research in Child Development 57(6)*, 1-153

Snow, C. E., Dubber, C. and de Blauw, A. (1982) Routines in mother-child interaction. In L. Feagans and D. C. Farran (Eds) *The language of children reared in poverty: Implications for evaluation and intervention*. New York: Academic Press

Snow, C. (1984) Therapy as social interaction: Analyzing the context for language remediation. *Topics in Language Disorders 4(4)*, 72-85

Terdal, L.E., Jackson, R.H. and Garner, A.M. (1976) Mother-child interactions: A comparison between normal and developmentally delayed groups. In E.J. Mash, L.A. Hamerlynck and L.C. Handy (Eds.) *Behaviour Modification and Families*. New York: Brunner/Mazel

Viet, S.W., Allen G.J. and Chinsky J.M. (1976) Interpersonal interactions between institutionalised retarded children and their attendants. *American Journal of Mental Deficiency 80*, 535- 542

Ware, J. (1987) Providing Education for Children with Profound and Multiple Learning Difficulties: A Survey of Resources and an Analysis of Staff-Pupil Interactions in Special Care Units. Unpublished PhD Thesis University of London Institute of Education

Ware, J. (1994) Classroom organisation In J. Ware (Ed) *Educating Children with Profound and Multiple Learning Difficulties*. London: David Fulton.

Ware, J. and Evans, P. (1986) Interactions between profoundly handicapped pupils in a special care class. In J. Berg and J. De Jong (Eds) *Science and Service in Mental Retardation*. London: Methuen.

Ware, J., Morahan, M., O'Connor, S. and Anderson, M. (1992) Interactions between pupils with severe learning difficulties and non-handicapped peers. *British Journal of Special Education Research Section 19(4)*, 153-158

Watson, J.S. and Ramey, C.T. (1972) Reactions to response-contingent stimulation in early infancy. *Merrill-Palmer Quarterly 18*, 219-227

Wilcox, M. J., Kouri, T.A. and Caswell, S. (1990) Partner sensitivity to communication behavior of young children with developmental disabilities. *Journal of Speech and Hearing Disorders 55*, 679-693

Wishart, J. (1991) Motivational deficits and their relation to learning difficulties in young children with Down's syndrome. In J. Watson (Ed) *Innovatory Practice and Severe Learning Difficulties*. Edinburgh: Moray House Publications. Holyrood Road, Edinburgh EH8 8AQ

Yoder, P. J. (1987) Relationship between degree of infant handicap and clarity of infant cues. *American Journal of Mental Deficiency 91*, 639-641.

Index